THE
TEDDY
BEAR
COMPANION™
Volume II

by
Dee Hockenberry
photos by
Tom Hockenberry

COWLES
Enthusiast Media

Dee Hockenberry is the author of seven other books on collectibles and contributes to three teddy bear magazines on a regular basis. She is particularly well known in the field of Steiff and often lectures on the subject. Along with a partner, Dee has a well-established business selling teddies, other soft toys and related products. Beginning her career as a teddy bear designer in 1980, she still finds time to supply shops both in the United States and abroad with her specialty.

Tom, Dee's husband, does all of the photography. They live in a house inhabited by three cats, teddy bears galore and other toys. They are parents of two grown children.

AUTHOR'S NOTE: I wish to thank the following collectors who graciously allowed us to photograph their treasures: Sam Annalora, Doris Barrows, Rita Casey (artist), Susan Cincinelli, Cynthia's Country Store, Michelle Daunton, Donna Felger, Francoise, Ray, Genevieve and Adam Flint, Elaine Lehn, Vince Mirro, Ronnie Morrison, Sherry Norman, Lorraine Oakley and Barbara and Dennis Yusa.

I am also indebted to the talented artists and dedicated Arctophiles who sent photographs. They are Debbie Anton, Dottie Ayers, Regina Brock, Genie Buttitta, Penny Chalmers, Nancy Crowe, Gloria Franks, Chester Freeman, Diane Gard, Ronwyn Graham, Jo Greeno, Billee Henderson, Elke Kraus, Cindy Martin, Joan Mears, Marion Mehling, Fred Slayter, Michi and Hiro Takahashi, Anne-Marie Van Gelder, Jan Vennix (all of the New Zealand artists), Beverly White, Mort and Evelyn Wood, David Worland, Ken Yenke and a private collector.

I also owe a special thank you to David Miller and Cowles Magazines, Inc., for their faith in me and to my editor, Donna H. Felger.

And lastly and most importantly, my husband, Tom, without whose hours of photographing, typing and support I could not accomplish anything.

My sincerest thanks to you all and may you always have a teddy bear close by to warm your hearts.

Table of Contents

THE TEDDY BEAR COMPANION
VOLUME II
©1996 COWLES MAGAZINES INC.,
4 High Ridge Park, Stamford CT 06905
(203) 321-1778

Library of Congress Cataloging-in-Publication Data

Hockenberry, Dee.
    The teddy bear companion / by Dee Hockenberry.
        p.   cm.
    Includes indexes.
    ISBN 0-86573-969-2 (v. 2 : softcover).
    1. Teddy bears.   I. Title.
    NK8740.H62 1995
    688.7'24--dc20   95-13998

COWLES
Enthusiast Media

Steiff Dicky Teddy Bear

INTRODUCTION

The Steiff Company in Germany and the Ideal Novelty and Toy Company in America both lay claim to producing the first teddy bear. Each firm's version appeared on the market at approximately the same time and while both bears were fully articulated, any resemblance stops there.

Steiff has always given meticulous attention to the detail of their teddies and animals. The bears have wonderful proportions and expressive faces and, while conformation changed over the years, they remain appealing. The animals are so finely wrought that one can almost see the musculature. Identification began around 1904 with an elephant-embossed silver-colored button in the left ear. This logo progressed with a blank button, followed by a button with Steiff letters printed (with a trailing final F) to a raised script, an indented script and ultimately, beginning in the 1970s, to a brass one. Chest tags came into vogue in the 1920s with a white metal-rimmed circle and this, too, changed over the years. To fully see the advancement, it is necessary to study the photographs and descriptions.

Gebrüder Bing, also of Germany, produced toys from 1860 to 1932. The first teddy appeared in 1906. This firm also used a metal button, the first in the form of an ear clip and then settling on a round button attached to the teddy's side. This enterprise led the field in amazing mechanicals.

Other German soft toys the collector will encounter are those made by Schuco (1912-1976), Kersa (1925 on), Gebrüder Hermann (1948 on) and Hermann Spielwaren (1979 on). Hermann began operations in 1913 and these two firms are descendants. Lesser known companies include Althans, Anker, Berg, Eli, Erle, Fechter, Helvetic, Jopi and Petz. While the names are perhaps not as prominent, they produced lovely and collectible products and should not be overlooked.

The Ideal Novelty and Toy Company ceased making teddy bears in 1982 when it was acquired by CBS. The earliest teddies (pre-1910) have adorable quirky faces and the longer mohair and body limbs associated with bears of this era. By 1920, football-shaped torsos and more bristly mohair was employed. Unfortunately, Ideal did not use identifying labels; therefore, judgment must be made by studying examples and even then, "attributed to" is probably a safer assumption.

American companies in the pre-1910 period include Aetna, Bruin, Columbia, Hecla and Strauss. Joining the field at a later date are Applause, Character, Commonwealth, Dakin, Knickerbocker, North American Bears and the Vermont Teddy Bear Company. Of course, there are many more unidentifiable, and others too numerous to list in operation today making quality products.

Great Britain is certainly one of the three major countries that began developing their own special teddy bears in the early stages of the toy's beginnings. Some of the companies that made lovely examples and are no longer in business are Farnell, W. J. Terry, Harwin, Jungle Toys, Twyford, Chiltern Arlesford, Nisbet, Pedigree, Peacock and Wendy Boston. Still producing teddies are Chad Valley, Dean's, Merrythought, Little Folk and Canterbury Bears. Most of the firms used labels that, if still intact, are certainly an identification aid. However, each country seems to have its own style and collectors will find that once they have studied or handled enough examples, they will be able to tell the country of origin, if not the maker.

In addition to the "Big Three," other countries whose bears you might encounter are Australia, Austria, China, Japan, France, Italy and Switzerland.

Teddy bear shows, where new commercial and artist designs can be purchased, are a fairly recent phenomena, appearing in about the last twenty years.

Prices are much less than those of vintage creatures, thus insuring that everyone can find something dear to their heart in an affordable price range.

Caring for new collectibles should not present any problems. Periodic inspections and frequent dusting should suffice. When attending to older bears and animals, care should be taken to see that they are free of moths and other foreign matter. Cleaning and repairs are best left to experts. Help in this field can be found via your favorite dealer or retail shop.

How often have dealers of antique bears been asked what they know about a particular teddy? The answer is, "constantly." Those that deal on a regular basis can normally supply the pertinent facts of age, country of origin and often the maker. Beyond that, anything else is rarely known. When a bruin is offered for sale by the original owner or relative, this information is known as the provenance. It is lovely and quite a thrill to be in possession of this data and certainly, the reference should be preserved, although in most instances, this should not affect the monetary value. However, this position can be reversed if the provenance is of great human or historical significance.

One of the most stunning examples of this occurred on December 5, 1994, at Christie's Auction House In South Kensington, London. The collection of Lt. Col. T. R. Henderson (1904-1990) was offered for sale and drew worldwide attention. Colonel "Bob," as he was known to those who loved him, was an arctophile extraordinaire and also the creator of the philanthropic organization "Good Bears of the World." Founded in Edinburgh in the early 1970s, Good Bears of the World is still viable, sending teddies to sick, injured and disturbed children who need this loving comfort. Lot number 32 was one of the major attractions, since this 18-inch, center-seam, cinnamon Steiff, circa 1904, bear had been Colonel Bob's lifelong companion. *Teddy Girl* (pictured at right) was offered along with a miniature photo album, several books and periodicals and twelve photos of the colonel and his special friend.

To say the bidding, when this bear reached the auction table, was exciting is a gross understatement. The air became charged with electricity as the final hammer-down price reached 110,000 English pounds (including buyer's premium). At the time of exchange, this translated to $171,600 – a new record and surely one that will not be broken for a long time. I was privileged to learn of the event immediately since friends in London phoned with the exciting news. A call from Steiff U.S.A. followed, for they were obviously elated, as well.

What does this mean to the bear world in general? The downside is that a few uninformed individuals will mistakenly think that every teddy bear they own is worth thousands of dollars. The most important and uplifting fact is that it verifies that teddy bears continue to be an important collecting hobby and the possibility exists in the potential for good investment. Of course, this is a special case and *Teddy Girl* will reside in a Japanese museum for all to admire. Therefore, the best advice is still to buy the best and, most importantly, the teddy that you really love and want to share your life with.

The prices in this book are meant to be a guide to aid the collector and are not to be taken as absolute. In most instances, the value given is for the particular animal in the photograph and what it recently sold for. When purchasing a like or similar example, remember the price can go up or down with the variables. Price can also depend on that indefinable something called "appeal," and that is, of course, in the

Steiff Teddy Girl • 18 inches

Curly cinnamon mohair; shoe-button eyes; replaced felt pads; excelsior stuffed;
all jointed; center head seam; lifelong companion of Colonel T. R. Henderson;
sold at Christie's Auction, London, in December 1994; pre-1907.
Marks: None
Price: $171,600
(sold with various Henderson photographs, books and memorabilia)
Courtesy of Steiff U.S.A.

eye of the beholder. We all recognize that when a teddy's face cries out to us, caution and expediency are gone with the wind. While the prices given are as accurate as possible, neither the author nor the publisher assumes any responsibility for losses occurred when either buying or selling.

NOTE: Sometimes a bear or an animal is issued with clothes, a ribbon or other accessory but in most cases, especially on old teddy bears, these items have been added for decorative purposes and are not original.

For more detailed and comprehensive information on companies, labels and other aspects of collecting and caring for teddy bears and animals, please refer to the Introduction in Volume I of *The Teddy Bear Companion*. You will find that the items identified and photographed in each volume are totally different and fresh. We intend to introduce future works periodically with collectibles that have not appeared in previous editions. Thus, the collector will have a new and exciting addition to add to their *Teddy Bear Companion* library in encyclopedic form.

The author would welcome hearing from any reader who has teddies not found in these volumes. Write in care of the publisher. The sharing and fellowship in the Bear World is what makes this pursuit such a "Happy Hunting" experience.

The conformation, choice of materials for all components and the method used for identification changed gradually over the years that the teddy bear has been in existence. These variations can best be seen by studying the photographs and descriptions for each bruin. Every country had (and has) its own choice of design, as well, and with enough handling of teddy bears, one can become proficient in telling the difference.

American Teddy Bear • 11 inches

Gold mohair; glass eyes; felt pads; fabric nose; excelsior stuffed; manufacturer unknown; circa 1907.
Marks: None
Price: $1,000-$1,500

American Teddy Bear • 12½ inches

Gold mohair; deep-set shoe-button eyes; felt pads; excelsior stuffed; attributed to Ideal; circa 1908.
Marks: None
Price: $1,100-$1,150

Steiff
Teddy Bear
24 inches

Cinnamon mohair; shoe-button eyes; felt
pads; excelsior stuffed; all jointed; near mint;
circa 1906.
Marks: Printed FF button
Price: $8,000 up
David Worland Collection

Steiff
Rod Bear
16 inches

Apricot mohair; shoe-button
eyes; felt pads; five claws;
excelsior stuffed; (missing
sealing wax nose and
replaced by embroidery; the
mouth has also been redone);
all jointed; near mint; 1902.
Marks: Elephant button
Price: $15,000 up

Steiff Teddy
Bear
24 inches

Gold mohair; shoe-button eyes;
felt pads; excelsior stuffed; all
jointed; mint; circa 1904.
Marks: Blank button
Price: $8,000 up
Evelyn and Mort Wood Collection

Steiff Teddy Bear • 24 inches

Apricot mohair; shoe-button eyes; felt pads; excelsior stuffed; center head
seam; wears old but not original bracelet; desirable size, color and expression;
near mint; circa 1906.
Marks: None
Price: $7,400-$7,500

American Teddy Bear 16 inches

Gold mohair; felt pads; shoe-button eyes; excelsior stuffed; all jointed; near mint; maker unknown; circa 1906.
Marks: None
Price: $1,350-$1,400

Steiff Teddy Bear 24 inches

Beige mohair; shoe-button eyes; felt pads; "cone" nose; excelsior stuffed; all jointed; excellent condition; circa 1907.
Marks: FF button
Price: $7,500-$8,000
Anne-Marie Van Gelder Collection

American Teddy Bear • 12 inches

Pale gold mohair; felt pads; shoe-button eyes; excelsior stuffed; all jointed; attributed to Ideal; circa 1906.

Marks: None

Price: $950 up

Steiff Teddy Bear • 16 inches

Pale gold mohair; felt pads; shoe-button eyes; excelsior stuffed; all jointed; near mint; circa 1907. Marks: Blank button

Price: $3,000

Steiff Teddy Bear • 16 inches

Cinnamon mohair; felt pads; shoe-button eyes; excelsior stuffed; all jointed; excellent condition; circa 1907. Marks: Blank button

Price: $2,700 *Dennis Yusa Collection*

Aetna Teddy Bear 20 inches

Gold mohair; felt pads; glass eyes; cork stuffed; charming suit made for him, probably by original owner; near mint; circa 1907. Marks: None

Price: $1,450-$1,500

Steiff Teddy Bear • 20 inches

White mohair that has silvered with age; shoe-button eyes; felt pads; center head seam; felt under nose and pads; softly stuffed excelsior; all jointed; circa 1907. (Note: This bear has been widely photographed and has universal appeal. Therefore, he would bring a higher price than the average 20-inch comparable teddy.)

Marks: None

Price: $6,000 up

American Teddy Bear • 20 inches

White mohair; shoe-button eyes; replaced felt pads; excelsior stuffed;
all jointed; excellent condition; probably Hecla.
Marks: None
Price: $2,000-$2,100

American Teddy Bear • 20 inches

Off-white mohair; shoe-button eyes; felt pads (cardboard lined); excelsior stuffed; all jointed; near mint; attributed to Hecla; circa 1908.
Marks: None
Price: $1,500 up

American Teddy Bear • 22 inches

Gold mohair; shoe-button eyes; felt pads (cardboard lined); excelsior stuffed; all jointed; near mint; attributed to Aetna; circa 1907.
Marks: None
Price: $2,000 up

American Teddy Bear • 16 inches

Gold mohair; shoe-button eyes; felt pads; excelsior stuffed; all jointed; excellent condition; maker unknown; circa 1907.
Marks: None
Price: $900 up

American Musical Teddy Bear • 16 inches

White mohair; clipped muzzle; glass eyes; felt pads; excelsior stuffed; all jointed; bellows music box; mint; circa 1920.
Marks: None
Price: $1,500 up

Evelyn and Mort Wood Collection

American Teddy Bear
20 inches

Gold mohair; felt pads; shoe-button eyes;
sewn-on fabric nose; embroidered mouth
and five claws; excelsior stuffed; all jointed; excellent condition; probably an
Ideal bear; circa 1908.
Marks: None
Price: $1,250-$1,350

Steiff Teddy Bear
14 inches

Bright cinnamon mohair; shoe-button
eyes; felt pads; floss nose, mouth and
claws; excelsior but softly stuffed; mint;
circa 1908.
Marks: Blank button
Price: $2,500-$2,700

American Teddy Bear
13 inches

Tan mohair; shoe-button eyes; felt pads;
five claws; excelsior stuffed; all jointed;
good condition; maker unknown; circa
1909.
Marks: None
Price: $950-$1,000
Dennis Yusa Collection

Steiff Teddy Bear • 18½ inches

Gray mohair (probably originally brown); shoe-button eyes; felt pads;
excelsior stuffed; excellent condition; circa 1910.

Marks: FF button

Price: $3,500 up

Anne-Marie Van Gelder Collection

Steiff
Teddy Bear
8 inches

Tan mohair; shoe-button eyes; repaired
felt pads; excelsior stuffed; all jointed;
circa 1910.
Marks: None
Price: $450-$475

German
Teddy Bear
24 inches

Beige mohair; felt pads; shoe-button eyes;
excelsior stuffed; all jointed; excellent
condition; maker unknown; circa 1910.
Marks: None
Price: $1,600-$1,800
Joan Mears Collection

Steiff
Teddy Bear
20 inches

Gold mohair; shoe-button eyes; felt pads;
excelsior stuffed; all jointed; shows wear;
circa 1910.
Marks: Printed FF button
Price: $1,500-$1,700
Lorraine Oakley Collection

American Teddy Bear 12 inches

Brown coat wool; shoe-button eyes; nose and mouth restitched; flannel foot pads; excelsior stuffed; pronounced hump; jointed by wire; near mint; circa 1910.
Marks: None
Price: $225-$250
Doris Barrows Collection

Steiff Teddy Bears • 3½ inches

Nine teddies in various colors and conditions; eight are 1910 or earlier; second from left is circa 1920; (larger Steiff bear in center is circa 1910); some still retain their FF buttons.
Marks: As stated
Price: $450 up
(depending on color, condition, identification and facial appeal)
Joan Mears Collection

American Teddy Bear 11 inches

Tan mohair; shoe-button eyes; felt pads; reworked nose and mouth; excelsior stuffed; all jointed; excellent condition; circa 1910.
Marks: None
Price: $900 up

American Teddy Bear 17 inches

Tan mohair; clear glass eyes with black pupils; replaced felt pads; excelsior stuffed; unusual conformation; worn condition; circa 1910.
Marks: None
Price: $350-$375

English Teddy Bear 18 inches

White mohair; glass eyes; felt pads; jointed claws on front of paw pads; excelsior stuffed; all jointed; possibly made by Farnell; mint; circa 1910.
Marks: None
Price: $1,500 up
Joan Mears Collection

German Bing Teddy • 24 inches

Ivory mohair; glass eyes; felt pads; excelsior and kapok stuffed; all jointed; circa 1915.
Marks: None
Price: $5,000-$5,200

American Teddy Bear 18 inches

Short gold mohair; felt pads; excelsior stuffed; all jointed; showing wear; possibly Ideal; circa 1915.
Marks: None
Price: $425-$440
Sherry Norman Collection

German Teddy Bear 22 inches

Light brown mohair; glass eyes; felt pads; excelsior stuffed; all jointed; near mint; maker unknown; circa 1920.
Marks: None
Price: $1,600 up

German Teddy Bear 28 inches

Gold mohair; glass eyes; felt pads; excelsior stuffed; all jointed; excellent condition; maker unknown; circa 1915.
Marks: None
Price: $2,500 up
Evelyn and Mort Wood Collection

English Teddy Bear 15 inches

Tan mohair; glass eyes; felt pads; fat thighs; excelsior stuffed head and kapok body; all jointed; near mint; circa 1915.
Marks: None
Price: $550-$600
Doris Barrows Collection

American Teddy Bear 23 inches

White mohair; glass eyes; felt pads; excelsior stuffed; all jointed; excellent condition; circa 1920.
Marks: None
Price: $350-$400

American Teddy Bear 16 inches

Dark gold mohair; shoe-button eyes; felt pads; excelsior stuffed; all jointed; excellent condition; circa 1918.
Marks: None
Price: $250-$300
Courtesy of Sam Annalora

American Teddy Bear 23 inches

Gold mohair; glass eyes; felt pads; football-shaped body; excelsior stuffed; all jointed; mint; probably Ideal; circa 1918.
Marks: None
Price: $800-$850
Doris Barrows Collection

American Teddy Bear
23 inches

Tan mohair; glass eyes; felt pads; football-shaped body; excelsior stuffed; all jointed; worn; circa 1918.
Marks: None
Price: $375-$385

English Teddy Bear
17 inches

White mohair; felt pads; shoe-button eyes; brown floss nose, mouth and claws (note paw pattern often done on English bears and thought to be by Farnell); excelsior stuffed; some hair loss; clothes not original; circa 1919.
Marks: None
Price: $1,500-$1,550

Steiff Teddy Bear
16 inches

Gold mohair; glass eyes; felt pads; excelsior stuffed; all jointed; excellent condition; decoration added; circa 1920.
Marks: Printed FF button
Price: $1,900-$2,000

Steiff Teddy Bear
14 inches

Gold mohair; glass eyes; felt pads; excelsior stuffed;
all jointed; near mint; circa 1920.
Marks: Printed FF button
Price: $2,000 up

Steiff Teddy Bear
9½ inches

White mohair; glass eyes; felt pads; excelsior
stuffed; all jointed; excellent condition; circa
1920. Marks: Printed FF button
Price: $1,140-$1,250

Dennis Yusa Collection

English Teddy Bears • 22, 26 and 18 inches

Pale gold and off-white mohairs; glass eyes; felt pads; excelsior and kapok filled;
all jointed; near mint; made by Farnell; circa 1920.
Marks: 26-inch bear has tag on foot
Price: $1,500, $2,000 and $1,400 up
Evelyn and Mort Wood Collection

Schuco
Yes/No Teddy Bear
11 inches

Cream mohair with vermilion tipping;
clear glass eyes; rayon pads (replaced with
felt on feet); black floss nose and mouth;
excelsior stuffed; all jointed; worn; clothes
not original; circa 1925.
Marks: None
Price: $650-$700

Schuco Yes/No
Teddy Bear
14 inches

Gold mohair; shoe-button eyes; felt pads
(feet replaced); excelsior stuffed; all
jointed; shows wear; circa 1925.
Marks: None
Price: $650-$700

American
Teddy Bear
18 inches

Bright cinnamon mohair; glass eyes; velvet
pads; metal nose; excelsior and cotton
stuffed; all jointed; excellent condition;
made by Knickerbocker; circa 1925.
Marks: None
Price: $375
Francoise Flint and Family Collection

English Teddy Bear • 22 inches

Tan mohair; clipped snout; glass eyes; felt pads; joined claw stitches on front paws; excelsior stuffed; all jointed; made by Farnell; circa 1925.

Marks: None

Price: $1,400 up

Steiff
Clown Teddy Bear
11 inches

Brown tipped white mohair (tipping faded); glass eyes; felt pads; excelsior stuffed; all jointed; good condition; original ruff; hat missing; circa 1926.
Marks: Printed FF button
Price: $1,000 up
Francoise Flint and Family Collection

English
Teddy Bear
36 inches

Long curly rose mohair; felt pads; amber glass eyes; floss nose, mouth and claws; excelsior stuffed; all jointed; excellent condition; circa 1930.
Marks: None
Price: $1,500-$1,800

American
Teddy Bear
15 inches

Bright gold mohair; glass eyes; felt pads; excelsior and kapok stuffed; all jointed; possibly made by Gund; circa 1929.
Marks: None
Price: $450-$500
Ken Yenke Collection

Steiff Dicky Teddy Bear • 13 inches

Gold mohair with tan inset snout; embroidered claws, nose and smiling mouth (originally mouth was airbrushed to a greater smile – now faded); pads were once airbrushed colorfully, now felt recovered; excelsior stuffed; 1930. Although over 14,000 were made in gold and 11,000 in white, they are rare. The 1930 *Dicky* is shown with Steiff's 1985 limited edition replica.

Marks: Printed FF button

Price: $2,000-$10,000 depending on condition.

(A perfect example would probably bring more.)

English Teddy Bear • 18½ inches

Gold mohair; brown glass eyes; excelsior and kapok stuffed; felt pads;
all jointed; excellent condition; made by Farnell; circa 1930.
Marks: None
Price: $1,200

German Teddy Bear 20 inches

Gold mohair; felt pads; clear glass eyes; slight wear to pads; excelsior stuffed; all jointed; manufacturer unknown; circa 1935.
Marks: None
Price: $650-$750

American Teddy Bear 9½ inches

Brown mohair; felt pads; shoe-button eyes backed with felt; red tongue; soft stuffed; all jointed; excellent condition; circa 1935.
Marks: Label in ear "Character Norwich, Conn."
Price: $75-$80
Doris Barrows Collection

American Teddy Bear 28 inches

Brown mohair; felt pads; glass eyes; excelsior stuffed; all jointed; excellent condition; growler; Knickerbocker; circa 1935.
Marks: None
Price: $900-$1,000

English Teddy Bear 18 inches

Gold mohair; brown glass eyes; excelsior stuffed head; kapok stuffed body; rexine pads; all jointed; near mint; made by Chad Valley; circa 1937.
Marks: Label on foot
Price: $300-$325

American Teddy Bear 13 inches

Brown mohair; velvet inset muzzle and pads; plastic eyes; cloth nose; soft stuffed; all jointed; excellent condition; Knickerbocker; circa 1945.
Marks: None
Prices: $75-$85

American Teddy Bear 16 inches

White mohair; glass eyes; felt pads; metal nose; excelsior and cotton stuffed; all jointed; Knickerbocker; circa 1935.
Marks: None
Price: $195-$225
Ronnie Morrison Collection

American Teddy Bear 16 inches

Brown alpaca; glass eyes; felt pads; excelsior stuffed; all jointed; excellent condition; manufacturer unknown; circa 1940.
Marks: None
Price: $350-$400
Susan Cincinelli Collection

English Teddy Bear 20 inches

Gold mohair; shoe-button eyes; felt pads; soft stuffed; rexine nose; all jointed; appears to be late 1930s and of English origin.
Marks: None
Price: $450-$500

English Teddy Bear 16 inches

Long gold mohair; brown velvet pads; clear glass eyes; excelsior and kapok stuffed; all jointed; shows wear on face; made by Chiltern; circa 1940.
Marks: None
Price: $350-$400

Teddy Bear • 17 inches

Lavender mohair, faded; clear glass eyes; linen-like pads; soft stuffed; all jointed; maker unknown; circa 1940.
Marks: None
Price: $350-$400

Schuco
Teddy Bear
15 inches

Tan mohair; glass eyes; clipped mohair pads and muzzle; excelsior stuffed; all jointed; good condition; circa 1945.
Marks: None
Price: $300 up
Francoise Flint and Family Collection

Pedigree
Teddy Bear
29 inches

Gold mohair; glass eyes backed by brown felt; velvet pads; kapok stuffed; all jointed; wind-up music box on back; circa 1945.
Marks: Tagged "Pedigree/made in Ireland"
Price: $700-$750

Steiff
Teddy Baby
9 inches

Brown mohair with tan muzzle and feet; glass eyes; felt pads; open mouth; excelsior stuffed; collar and bell; mint; circa 1948.
Marks: Raised button; U S Zone tag
Price: $925

Steiff Teddyli • 9 inches

Mohair head, feet and paws; open felt mouth; unjointed; felt and cotton clothes; squeaker; mint; circa 1948.

Marks: Raised button; U S Zone tag

Price: $1,500 up

Ken Yenke Collection

Schuco Yes/No Music Teddy Bear • 17 inches

Tan mohair; glass eyes; felt pads; excelsior stuffed; all jointed;
music box wound in stomach; mint; 1948.
Marks: Plastic "Tricky" tag
Price: $1,900 up

Steiff Teddy Baby • 3½ inches

Brown mohair; tan velvet muzzle and feet; glass eyes; excelsior stuffed;
all jointed; mint; circa 1950.
Marks: Raised button; bear head chest tag
Price: $1,100
Francoise Flint and Family Collection

Hermann Teddy Bear 24 inches

Caramel mohair; clipped muzzle; glass eyes; excelsior stuffed; felt pads; growler; large tummy; all jointed; mint; circa 1948.

Marks: None

Price: $800-$850

Courtesy of Marion Hermann Mehling, Gebr. Hermann KG

Steiff Teddy Bears • 3½ inches

Gold mohair; black bead eyes; no paw pads; excelsior stuffed; mint condition; bow and bell not original; circa 1950.

Marks: Raised button on left bear; no ID on right bear

Price: $195 to $250 each

Steiff Teddy Bear • 15 inches

White mohair; glass eyes; felt pads; brown nose, mouth and claws; excelsior
stuffed; all jointed; near mint; circa 1950.
Marks: Raised button
Price: $650-$700

Steiff
Teddy Bear
13 inches

White mohair; glass eyes; excelsior stuffed; all jointed; mint; circa 1950.
Marks: Raised button
Price: $500 up
Susan Cincinelli Collection

German
Teddy Bear
11 inches

Yellow and cream plush; inset snout; glass googly eyes; excelsior stuffed; all jointed; good condition; circa 1950.
Marks: None
Price: $65-$75
Doris Barrows Collection

German
Teddy Bear
22 inches

Tan mohair; clipped mohair muzzle and pads; glass eyes; rust floss nose and mouth; soft stuffed; all jointed; manufacturer unknown; circa 1950.
Marks: None
Price: $250-$300
Doris Barrows Collection

American Teddy Bear 17 inches

White mohair; glass eyes; felt pads; soft stuffed; all jointed; manufacturer unknown; circa 1950.
Marks: None
Price: $250-$275

American Teddy Bear 8 inches

Gold and white plush; glass eyes; soft stuffed; squeaker; good condition; possibly made by Character; circa 1950.
Marks: None
Price: $30-$35

American Teddy Bear 19 inches

Brown and gold plush; plastic eyes and tongue; leather nose; excelsior stuffed; all jointed; unknown maker; circa 1950.
Marks: None
Price: $75-$80

Doris Barrows Collection

American Teddy Bear 16 inches

Gold mohair; glass eyes; felt pads; soft stuffed; all jointed; bellows music box activated by pressing stomach; shows wear; manufacture unknown; circa 1950.
Marks: None
Price: $250-$300

English Teddy Bear 9½ inches

Off-white mohair; brown glass eyes; rex-ine pads (paint worn off); soft stuffed; all jointed; shows some wear; circa 1950.
Marks: None
Price: $225-$250

Schuco Yes/No Teddy Bear 16 inches

Tan mohair; glass eyes; felt pads (repaired); excelsior stuffed; all jointed; some fading and discoloration on one side; circa 1950.
Marks: None
Price: $695-$750

Schuco
Yes/No Teddy Bear
13 inches

Tan mohair; clear glass eyes painted
brown on back; felt pads; black floss
mouth, nose and claws; excelsior stuffed;
minor mohair loss; circa 1950.
Marks: None
Price: $650-$700

Steiff
Zotty Bear
10 inches

Brown frosted mohair; apricot mohair chest plate;
glass eyes; open felt mouth and pads; excelsior
stuffed; all jointed; excellent condition;
circa 1955.
Marks: None
Price: $175-$200
Ronnie Morrison Collection

Swiss
Teddy Bear
14 inches

Tan mohair; glass eyes; felt pads; soft and
hard stuffed; all jointed; internal wind-up
music box; head turns from side to side
when music plays; good condition;
manufactured by Mutzli; circa 1950.
Marks: None
Price: $300 up

Teddy Bear
13 inches

Pale gold mohair; glass eyes; gold felt
foot pads; soft and excelsior stuffed; all
jointed; near mint; manufacturer
unknown; circa 1950.
Marks: None
Price: $100-$125
Doris Barrows Collection

Hermann
Teddy Bears
24 and 14 inches

Long cream mohair with brown tipping;
inset short mohair muzzles; glass eyes; felt
pads; excelsior stuffed; growlers;
all jointed; mint; circa 1953.
Marks: None
Price: $800-$850 (24 inches)
      $350-$400 (14 inches)
Courtesy of Marion Hermann Mehling,
Gebr. Hermann KG

Steiff
Cosy Teddies
11 inches

White Dralon with tan chest plate;
brown Dralon with white chest plate;
clipped muzzles with open felt mouths;
plastic eyes; white bear circa 1970;
brown bear circa 1955.
Marks: Raised script and incised script
buttons; bear head or split tags
Price: $155-$165 each

Steiff Teddy Bear • 17 inches

Caramel mohair; glass eyes; felt pads; excelsior stuffed; all jointed;
mint; circa 1955.
Marks: Raised button; bear head chest tag
Price: $600-$650

Steiff Teddy Bear • 8 inches

Gold mohair; glass eyes; felt pads; excelsior stuffed; all jointed; original ribbon;
mint; circa 1955.
Marks: Raised button; bear head chest tag
Price: $350

Steiff Teddy Bear • 6 inches

Gold mohair; glass eyes; no pads; excelsior stuffed; all jointed;
excellent condition; circa 1955.
Marks: None
Price: $195-$225

Dennis Yusa Collection

Steiff
Teddy Bear
3½ inches

Tan mohair; bead eyes; excelsior stuffed;
all jointed; near mint; circa 1955.
Marks: Chest tag
Price: $325-$350

Hermann Teddy Bear • 14 inches

Brown mohair; inset muzzle; glass eyes; replaced felt pads; excelsior stuffed; all
jointed; knit suit not original; excellent condition; circa 1955. Marks: None
Price: $275-$300

German Teddy Bear • 14 inches

Tan mohair; inset muzzle; glass eyes; replaced pads; excelsior stuffed; all jointed;
dress not original; shows wear; circa 1955. Marks: None
Price: $95-$100

Barbara Yusa Collection

Hermann Teddy Baby 15 inches

Tan mohair; glass eyes; inset snout; open mouth; clipped and airbrushed feet; excelsior stuffed; all jointed; replaced collar; mint; circa 1957.
Marks: None
Price: $450-$500
Doris Barrows Collection

German Teddy Bear 20 inches

Long tipped mohair; glass eyes; inset shaved snout; felt pads; excelsior stuffed; all jointed; near mint; possibly Eli Puppen Und Spieltiere; circa 1955.
Marks: None
Price: $200-$225
Doris Barrows Collection

German Teddy Bear
11 inches

Tan mohair; glass eyes; sheared mohair foot pads; felt hand pads stitched like fingers; red felt tongue; excelsior stuffed; all jointed; replaced weskit; possibly Grisly; circa 1955.
Marks: None
Price: $80-$85
Doris Barrows Collection

chuco
erlin Bear
3 inches

Brown mohair over metal; black metal eyes; all jointed; wears a Berlin banner nd metal crown; mint; circa 1955.
Marks: None
Price: $175-$200

teiff
osy Teddy Bear
inches

Plush; glass eyes; felt pads with airbrushing on feet; open felt mouth; jointed head and arms; 1957 only.
Marks: None
Price: $90-$95

Steiff
Zotty Bear
8 inches

Tan frosted mohair; apricot chest plate; glass eyes; open felt mouth; excelsior stuffed; wearing red and white romper suit; circa 1960. Marks: Bear head chest tag

Price: $240-$250

Steiff Petsy Bears • 14, 11 and 8 inches

Tan, gold and white woolly plush; glass eyes; velour pads; soft stuffed; all jointed; excellent condition; circa 1960.
Marks: Incised button on gold bear

Price: $175 (14 inches) $125 (11 inches) $100 (8 inches)

Dennis Yusa Collection

Steiff Zotty Bear • 11 inches

Tan frosted mohair; apricot chest plate; glass eyes; open felt-lined mouth; all jointed; signed on foot by Jorg Junginger, great-grandnephew of Margarete Steiff; near mint; circa 1960.

Marks: None

Price: $350

Steiff Zotty Bears • 6½ inches

Same description as 11-inch bear; desirable and hard-to-find size.

Marks: None

Price: $225

Steiff
Teddy Bear
10 inches

Tan mohair; glass eyes; felt pads; excelsior stuffed; all jointed; dressed and sold by F A O Schwarz; excellent condition; shown with Schwarz box; circa 1960. Marks: F A O Schwarz plastic hang tag
Price: $325 up

American Roly Poly Bear • 8 inches

Plush head; cotton snout, inner ears, paws and clothes; swivel head; pasted-on felt eyes; musical; made by Fisher Price; circa 1960.
Marks: "F. P." on bib; sewn-on tag on reverse side
Price: $35-$45

American Teddy Bear • 8 inches

Plush; glass eyes; yarn nose; soft stuffed; nonjointed; probably made by Character; circa 1960. Marks: None
Price: $10-$15

Schuco
Bigo Bello
Soccer Player
12 inches

Mohair; wired limbs; plastic eyes and nose;
soft stuffed; nonremovable clothes;
wearing Adidas shoes; circa 1960.
Marks: Paper hang tag
Price: $95-$100
Lorraine Oakley Collection

Lambskin
Teddy Bear
14 inches

Real skins; glass eyes; plastic nose; leather
pads; soft filled; all jointed; mint; appears to
be English or Australian; circa 1965.
Marks: None
Price: $150-$175

Fechter Teddy Bear 12 inches

Silver tipped brown mohair; brown tipped inset snout and pads; gold chest plate and inner ears; glass eyes; excelsior stuffed; all jointed; original red ribbon; mint; circa 1965.
Marks: None
Price: $195-$200

Grisly Teddy Bear • 12 inches

Gold mohair; inset muzzle; glass eyes; mohair pads; soft stuffed; all jointed; squeaker; original ribbon; mint; circa 1960.
Marks: Metal button on chest; label in arm seam; hang tag
Price: $125-$135

Grisly Teddy Bear • 9 inches

Gold mohair; inset muzzle; glass eyes; felt pads; soft and hard stuffed; all jointed; original ribbon; mint; circa 1968. Marks: Label in arm seam
Price: $95-$100
Vince Mirro Collection

Steiff
Floppy Teddy
13 inches

Pale cinnamon plush; plastic eyes; foam filled; tissue mint; circa 1974. Marks: Incised button; stock tag; split chest tag; hang tag
Price: $135-$145

Paddington Bear
17 inches

Gold plush with black ears; black plastic eyes; soft stuffed; felt hat and duffle coat; vinyl boots; mint; made by Eden Toys; 1977. Marks: Boot bottom "Eden 1977"
Price: $95-$100

Steiff
Toldi Teddy Bear
15 inches

Brown plush; plastic eyes; velour pads; nonjointed; blue cotton dress; mint; circa 1974.
Marks: Incised button; split chest tag
Price: $165-$175

Steiff
Toldi Teddy Bear
11 inches

Light brown and tan plush; plastic eyes; plush pads; very soft stuffed; baby item; 1980s.
Marks: Brass button; split chest tag
Price: $95-$100

Chinese Teddy Bear
15 inches

Tan mohair; plastic eyes; felt pads; hard stuffed; all jointed; made in China; circa 1980.
Marks: None
Price: $70-$75

Steiff Zotty Bears
10 and 12 inches

Brown tipped mohair; inset snouts; plastic eyes; open velour mouths and pads; foam filled; nonjointed; mint; late 1970s and 1980s.
Marks: Brass button on small bear; incised on left; split chest tags
Price: $95-$125 each

Teddy Bear
4 inches

Short pale gold mohair; bead eyes; hard stuffed; all jointed; sweater appears to be original; manufacturer unknown; circa 1980.
Marks: None
Price: $25-$30
Barbara Yusa Collection

English
Teddy Bear
18 inches

Brown plush; plastic eyes and nose; velvet pads;
soft stuffed; all jointed; made by Little Folks,
Devon, England; 1983.
Marks: Paper hang tag; brass pendant
on chain
Price: $100-$125

English
Unjointed Teddy Bear
20 inches

Tan plush head; plastic eyes and mouth;
velour and polyester clothes form body;
vinyl boots; permanently bent legs; soft
stuffed; mint; circa 1982.
Marks: Sewn-on label "By Casa Roma of
Lincolnshire, England"
Price: $200-$250

Steiff
Original Teddy Bears
7 and 14 inches

Mohair with clipped mohair on muzzles and
around the eyes; plastic eyes; velour pads; all
jointed; growlers; mint; a staple in the line
since the 1960s; identification reflects that
these are from the 1980s.
Marks: Brass buttons; split chest tags
Price: $95-$145 each

Steiff Teddy Bear Head Pin • 1¼ inches

Mohair head which came in colors of gold, caramel, brown and white; to be worn as a brooch; in box; 1980s.

Steiff Bendy Bear • 3½ inches

Brown mohair; bead eyes; bendable limbs; 1980s.
Marks: Brass buttons; split chest tag
Price: $35-$45 each

Steiff Display Petsy Bear 33 inches

Tan silky plush; plastic eyes; soft stuffed; all jointed; mint; 1980s.
Marks: Brass button; split chest tag; hang tag
Price: $550-$600

Steiff Petsy Bear 10 inches

Tan silky plush; plastic eyes; soft stuffed; mint; 1980s.
Marks: Brass button; split chest tag
Price: $125

Young Bully Bear 12 inches

Gold mohair; plastic eyes; velour pads; soft stuffed; all jointed; cotton beret and tunic; Bully Bear pin back button; mint-in-box; inspired by Peter Bull; made by English House of Nisbet; limited edition of 5,000; 1980s. Marks: Sewn-in tag on side and on foot; paper hang tag
Price: $75-$80

Nisbet Sailor Girl Teddy Bear 15 inches

Brown alpaca; plastic eyes; dressed in white sailor dress and cap; limited edition of 1,000 by English House of Nisbet.
Marks: Label sewn in seam; hang tag
Price: $175-$225
Barbara Yusa Collection

Steiff
Clifford Berryman Bear
13 inches

Brown mohair with white mohair inset face;
plastic googly eyes; airbrushed felt paws;
open mouth; made to commemorate the
85th anniversary of the cartoonist and the
Roosevelt cartoon bear; discontinued; 1987.
Marks: Brass button; yellow stock tag
Price: $250-$275

Paddington
Bear
4½ inches

Plush; plastic eyes and nose; felt hat and
coat; vinyl boots; paper sack; Eden Toys
Inc.; © 1987.
Marks: Label on coat; details on bottom
of bag
Price: $9-$10

Last
Elegant Bear
14 inches

Plush; unjointed; wearing shirt, tie and
jacket; produced by Gund, Inc.,
© Dennis Kyte; 1983.
Marks: Label in seam; paper hang tag
Price: $50-$60
Barbara Yusa Collection

Paddington 30th Anniversary Bear
11 inches

Plush standing bear; plastic eyes and nose; unjointed;
felt toggle coat and hat; vinyl boots; 1988.
Marks: "© Eden" on boots; Paddington label in leg seam; hang tag;
anniversary tag on hat
Price: $35-$40

Paddington 30th Anniversary Bear
9 inches

Plush; plastic eyes and nose; unjointed; knit sweater; felt hat; 1988.
Marks: Hang tag; label in leg seam; anniversary label on hat
Price: $25-$30

Sherry Norman Collection

American Teddy Bears 18 inches

Tan plush; plastic eyes; clipped plush pads; hard stuffed; original clothes; Bialosky teddy bears of 1980s production.
Marks: Tagged "Gund"
Price: $125-$150 each

English Teddy Bear 11 inches

Commemorative gift to a 1990 tour of England hosted by the Michauds; made by the Canterbury Co.; Henley-On-Thames outfit added a year later.
Marks: Label in seam
Price: $85 (without sweater)
Barbara Yusa Collection

Merrythought Teddy Bear 12½ inches

Made exclusively for Harrods Department Store, London; mohair head, paws and feet; dressed in green velvet to emulate the store's doorman; 1990s.
Marks: Merrythought hang tag
Price: $95-$100

While the term "Artists' Bears" has been recognized for less than twenty years, it is now a viable addition to the world of collecting. "World" is an apt name, for, although the movement had its genesis in the United States, there are now extremely talented artists worldwide. Prices given are what the teddies originally sold for. Add value for each succeeding year.

Genie Buttitta Teddy Tot Toy Shop
7, 7½, 6 and 3¾-inch bears

One-of-a-kind ensemble made for the 1st Disneyland Convention Auction in 1992; the shop is 15 inches tall and the shelves are filled with a variety of miniature toys.

Price: $950

Genie Buttitta Bear Buddy Necklace
3 inches

Shown left and right; pair of teddies dressed in vintage trims and lace; hung on cord for neck wear; open stock, but individually made; 1990 to present.

Price: $89

Genie Buttitta Shopping Days
5½ inches

Teddy bear with shopping cart; limited edition of three; 1990.

Price: $69

Genie Buttitta School Days
4½ inches

Vintage dressed with desk, books and apple; limited edition of five; 1990.

Price: $69

Regina Brock
Teddy Bear
22 inches

Designed with a unique process of weaving raw roving mohair onto linen; time-consuming and difficult; excelsior filled; discontinued method; one-of-a-kind; U.S.A.; 1990.
Price: $8,000

Wendy Brent
Bear on Fours
18 inches

Gold plush; glass eyes; molded nose; beautifully detailed felt saddle; limited edition of 25; U.S.A.; 1980s.
Marks: Sewn-in label; hang tag
Price: $300-$350

Wendy Brent
Bluebell
12 inches

White lamb's wool; blue glass eyes; padded and detailed leather paws; all jointed; silk and flower trim; limited edition of 50; U.S.A.; 1980s.
Marks: Sewn-in label; hang tag
Price: $250-$300

Beverly White
Laurel and Hardy Portrait Bears
30 inches

Toby award winners in three categories in 1992; the one-of-a-kind set was auctioned at the Disneyland Convention the same year; subsequently, a 15-inch size was created in an edition of 100. The portrait size is pictured with conceptual drawings; U.S.A.

Price: 30-inch pair $3,400 (at auction)
15-inch pair $995

Billee Henderson Violetta Teddy Bear
16 inches

Dense off-white mohair; violet glass eyes; felt pads; chintz dress; crinoline underskirt; silk violet crown and bouquet; limited edition of eight; U.S.A.; 1992.
Price: $325

The Paisley Bear And I in My Nightcap
21 inches

Green mohair; hair and beard woven in antique doll mohair; antique vest, socks, cap, shoes, glasses and watch; holding stocking with bear and antique doll; limited edition of five; by Fred Slayter and Joyce Martin; U.S.A.; 1992.
Price: $850

Gloria Franks Tubby • 17 inches

Antique rose and white curly mohair; glass eyes; panda styling; limited edition
of 50 (closed); company name "Goose Creek"; U.S.A.; 1993.

Price: $220

Trudy Yelland Teddy B and Teddy G Roly Polys 1½ inches

Artist's napped mini fabric; cotton; wire and bead trim; Canada; 1993.
Marks: Name tag on back
Price: $75 each

Ronwyn Graham Magician 3⅜ inches

Silvery gray artist's mini mohair; wearing Ultrasuede®, silk and broderie anglaise (eyelet embroidery) clothing; rabbit in hat; dove and wand; Toby nominee; limited edition of 25; Bambini Bears, Australia; 1993.
Price: 150 Australian dollars

Beverly White Ronald Portrait Bear 30 inches

Over 100 pieces of fabric used to create this one-of-a-kind teddy; swivel tilt armature in all four limbs; made for the Philadelphia Ronald MacDonald House Auction; U.S.A.; 1993

Price: $1,250

Elke Kraus Buffy Teddy Bear • 20 inches

Gold mohair; wearing large bow; limited edition of 30; Germany; 1990.
Price: No price available

Andrea Siggens
Barnaby Teddy Bear
19 inches

Tan mohair; glass eyes; tan felt pads;
number two of a limited edition of 50;
Great Britain; 1993.
Marks: Cloth tag sewn in back seam;
paper hang tag
Price: No price available
(gift to author)

Nicola Ann Peter
Teddy Bear
3 inches

Artists's mini fabric; bead trim; all
jointed; Great Britain; 1993.
Marks: Hang tag; enamel tree
Price: No price available
(gift to author)

Elizabeth and Jan
Vennix
Pink Meggs
14½ inches

Mohair; glass eyes; wearing colorful bow;
open edition; Beebs Bears, New Zealand;
1993.
Price: 200 New Zealand dollars

Cindy Martin
Sailor
Yesterbear
47 inches

Off-white mohair; needle-sculpted face; this large design was custom-made to accommodate the wearing of a 1940s sailor suit; U.S.A.; 1993.
Marks: Leather ID; paper hang tag
Price: $1,900

Nancy Crowe
Ann and Arthur
24 inches

Mohair; glass eyes; Ultrasuede® paws; Arthur wears a silk bow tie and antique glasses; Ann wears a vintage christening gown; one-of-a-kind; U.S.A.; 1993.
Price: $650 pair

Anne-Marie Van Gelder Erwin
12½ inches

Butterscotch mohair; old shoe-button eyes; plaid vest and bow tie; limited edition; Sunny Bears of Holland; 1993.

Price: $180

The Paisley Bear Rumford
20 inches

Gold mohair; corduroy pants and hat; trimmed in vintage paisley fabric; open edition; made by Fred Slayter and Joyce Martin; U.S.A.; 1993.

Price: $425

The Paisley Bear Sarah • 24 inches

Gray mohair; all jointed; vintage fabric clothing and hat; carries purse; 1994
Toby entry; made by Fred Slayter and Joyce Martin; U.S.A.
Marks: Label
Price: $1,000

Rita Casey
Raspberry
16 inches

Curly cotton bounce; Ultrasuede® paws; limited edition of ten; U.S.A.; 1994.
Price: $145

Anne-Marie Van Gelder
Benji and Celia
7 and 14½ inches

Dense ivory mohair; Benji has glass eyes, Celia has old shoe-button eyes; limited edition; Sunny Bears of Holland; 1994.
Price: $275 set

Chester Freeman
Teddy Bear
13 inches

Gold mohair; glass eyes; silk custom-made clothing; African mud cloth hat; one-of-a-kind; U.S.A.; 1994.
Price: $400

Diane Gard
Annie Shenanigan
18 inches

Gold mohair; violet glass eyes; plaid corduroy overalls; *Weisenheimer's* kid sister likes to surprise people with her jumping frog; open edition; U.S.A.; 1994.
Price: $249

Diane Gard
Anastasia
32 inches

Champagne mohair; hyacinth blue glass eyes; black velvet gown under a fur-trimmed cape; dove gray hat; "onyx" and "diamond" jewelry; vintage hat box; one-of-a-kind for the DisneyWorld 1994 Convention Auction; U.S.A.
Price: Unknown at writing

Cindy Martin
Toothsome Ted
Yesterbear
15 inches

Curly blended mohair; needle-sculpted face; dimensionally embroidered two bottom teeth and smiling mouth; open edition but as in all of this artists"'s teddies, the nature of all of the hand work renders each one unique; U.S.A.; 1994.
Marks: Leather ID; paper hang tag
Price: $500

Dee Hockenberry
Cornellia
18 inches

Off-white feather mohair; glass shoe-button style eyes; felt pads; all jointed; dressed in Cornell University baby-size shirt; special one-of-a-kind teddy for 1994 graduate from her mother; U.S.A.
Marks: Sewn-on label; hang tag
Price: $450

Jo Greeno
Bear Family
15, 14, 8 and 5 inches

Various mohair colors (collector's choice); Father is pellet stuffed with bent legs; Mother and children are hard stuffed; comes with individually hand-crafted chair; *Teddy Bear Times* award winner in undressed category; England; 1994.
Price: 500 British pounds

Penny Chalmers Hector • 14 inches

White German mohair; limited edition of five; company name "Little Charmers"; England; 1994.

Price: 95 British pounds

Ronwyn Graham
Lucille
24 inches

Mohair; wears lace collar and cameo; limited edition of ten; Bambini Bears; Australia; 1994.

Price: 330 Australian dollars

Elizabeth and Jan Vennix Teddy Bears
Hugo • 15½ inches
Brogio • 15½ inches
Aubrey • 11½ inches

Mohair; glass eyes; open editions; Beebs Bears, New Zealand; 1994.

Prices at Issue: 200, 185 and 175 New Zealand dollars

Nigel and Allie
Hanton Bears
Long Streak: 15½ inches
The Swede: 13 inches
Bobbie: 10 inches

Variety of mohair colors; open editions;
Edwardian Bears, New Zealand; 1994.
**Prices: 155, 120 and 110 New
Zealand dollars**
Courtesy of Jan Vennix

Fairy Chuckles
Prim Rosi
14 inches

Light beige, ¾-inch distressed German
Mohair; limited edition of five. As described
in the title, Rosi is making a prim face. She
wears a hand-dyed light rose pink blouse
with flowerlike sleeves on a romper dress;
hair ribbons are antique lace, made in
England; comes with producer's portrait.
Price: 38,000 Japanese yen

Fairy Chuckles
Bruno
14 inches

Gray, gold and hand-painted blue tipped
1-inch curly mohair; limited edition of
three; comes with producer's portrait.
Fairy Chuckles, husband-and-wife team
from Japan, Hiro and Michi Takahashi.
Price: 32,000 Japanese yen

When collecting teddy bears became such an important hobby and the craving for the earliest examples sometimes exceeded the supply, insightful companies started to reissue examples based on designs from previous eras. Many of these are offered in limited editions with certificates and presentation boxes.

Collectibles also include special products for a specific store and those models made only for a limited period of time. Examples in these categories include Steiff's editions for Harrods Department Store in London at Christmastime and the imaginative works of Robert Raikes and the North American Bear Co.

North American Ebearneezer Scrooge 19 inches

Green velour; wears nightshirt, glasses, cap and scarf; one of the V.I.B. Series; 1988. Marks: Hang tag
Price: $425 up

North American Elvis Bearsley 19 inches

Royal blue plush; gold lamé jumpsuit; carries guitar; one of the V.I.B. Series; 1984-1985. Marks: Hang tag
Price: $475 up

Barbara Yusa Collection

North American Running Bear
19 inches

Plush with made-on jogging suit and sneakers; the first bear made by North American Bear. This is the second series; © 1979.
Marks: Sewn-in label; hang tag
Price: $250 up
Dennis Yusa Collection

Steiff Richard Steiff Teddy Bear
12 inches

Gray mohair; named after his creator; bear pictured was signed by H.O. Steiff in 1983; presentation box; produced in 1982 in a limited edition of 20,000.
Marks: Brass button; white stock tag; hang tag on paw
Price: $350-$375

North American William Shakesbear
20 inches

Dark red velour; satin, velvet and felt clothes; near mint; 1981 to 1988.
Marks: Label in seam; hang tag
Price: $250 up

Steiff Mr. Cinnamon Bears
13 and 10 inches

Cinnamon mohair; made as open stock, but discontinued; replica of 1903 teddy bear; 1984.

Marks: Brass buttons; gold stock tags; (originally had hang tags)

Price: $350 up (13 inches) • **$250 up (10 inches)**

Steiff Ophelia 16 inches

White mohair; net ruff tied with ribbon; modeled after the bear in Michelle Clise's books; in box; 1984.

Marks: Brass button; hang tag

Price: $350-$375

Peter Bull and Teddy Bear • 8 inches

Memorial doll made by the House of Nisbet Ltd., England (no longer in business); *Peter* wears his favorite sweater and the bear has a scarf like the famous *Aloysius*; complete with paper tag; memorial booklet; presentation box; limited edition of 5,000; 1984.

Marks: As stated

Price: $150-$160

Steiff Teddy Baby and Wolf 11½ and 5 inches

Produced to celebrate the 85th anniversary of the Paul Wolff Toy Store in Giengen; bear and wolf are mohair and come in a box with certificate; box background is a sepia tone lithograph of the town and Wolff's store; mint-in-box; difficult to find on secondary market; limited edition of 1,000; 1988.
Marks: Brass buttons; chest tags
Price: $575 up

Steiff White Teddy Bear 12 inches

Made for F A O Schwarz Toy Store; presentation box with certificate; limited edition of 1,000; 1988.
Marks: Brass button; white stock tag; F A O Schwarz chest tag
Price: $250-$275

Steiff
Giengen Bear
20 inches

Gray mohair; plastic eyes; white felt
pads; largest of a set produced in 1986.
Marks: Brass button; Giengen
chest tag
Price: $500 up

North American
Blackbeard
20 inches

Black velour; colorfully dressed; parrot
on shoulder; (note <u>bear</u> skull and cross-
bones on headgear); mint; 1986-1990.
Marks: Label in seam; hang tag
Price: $250 up

Steiff
Teddy Rose
16 inches

Rose mohair; center head seam; replica
of a 1920 teddy bear; in box with certificate; limited edition of 10,000; 1987.
Marks: Brass button; white chest tag
Price: $350-$375

Steiff Dolly Bear 12 inches

White and yellow mohair; yarn ruff; error in color so only 240 pieces produced; mint; 1987.
Marks: Brass button; hang tag
Price: $395

Steiff Jackie Bears • 9 and 6 inches

Airbrushed tan mohair; plastic eyes; firmly stuffed; replicas of 1953 models produced in three sizes; in presentation boxes with certificates and *Jackie* booklets; 1987-1989.
Marks: Brass buttons; white stock tags; chest tags
Price: $185 (9 inches) • $145 (6 inches)

Steiff Muzzle Bear • 18 and 13 inches

White mohair; felt pads; plastic eyes; firmly stuffed; all jointed; leather muzzles and leads; in presentation boxes with certificates; three sizes introduced in limited editions in 1988-1990.

Marks: Brass buttons; white stock tags

Price: $550 (18 inches) • $300 (13 inches)

North American Muffy Vanderbear
7 inches

From the Nutcracker Collection; 1988.

Marks: Label in back seam; hang tag

Price: $450 up

Barbara Yusa Collection

Steiff Musical Bear 10 inches

Made for Harrods Department Store, London; wind-up music box plays "Brahms Lullaby"; in box; limited edition of 2,000; 1989.
Marks: Brass button; white stock tag; Harrods hang tag
Price: $325-$350

Robert Raikes Three Bears 7, 11 and 12 inches

On platform; box with certificate; limited edition of 7,500; distributed by Applause; 1989.
Marks: Hang tag; signed feet and platform
Price: $225 up

Steiff
Musical Bear
11½ inches

Made for Harrods Department Store, London; a version of Mr. *Cinnamon*; box with certificate; limited edition of 2,000; 1990.
Marks: White ear tag; hang tag
Price: $300-$325

Beaver Valley
Agatha Polar Bear
30 inches

White plush; padded and stitched leather pads and claws; molded nose and mouth; hinged mouth with teeth; poseable body; No. 5 of 25; U.S.A.; 1990.
Marks: Signed on foot
Price: $900 up

Steiff
Teddy Rose
10 inches

Pink mohair; glass eyes; limited edition of 8,000; 1990.
Marks: White chest tag; brass button; white stock tag
Price: $225-$250

Robert Raikes
Mother's Day Bears
5 and 10 inches

On wooden platform with wooden carriage for baby; dressed in lace-trimmed outfits with matching bonnets; limited edition of 7,500; The Good Company, a division of Applause; for Mother's Day 1990.
Marks: Hang tag; signed platform
Price: $200 up

Robert Raikes
Hilary
15 inches

A Camp Grizzly bear dressed appropriately; in box with certificate; limited edition of 7,500; Applause; 1990.
Marks: Hang tag; signed foot
Price: $200 up

Steiff
Dicky Bear
12 inches

Replica of a 1930s bear; note airbrushed pads; in box with certificate; limited edition of 7,000; 1992.
Marks: Brass button; white ear tag; replica chest tag
Price: $245

Steiff
Musical Teddy Bear
15 inches

Replica of a 1928 musical bear, operated by squeezing the stomach area; in box with certificate; limited edition of 8,000; 1992.
Marks: Brass button; white ear tag; replica chest tag
Price: $395

Merrythought
Teddy Bear
12 inches

Black mohair; plastic eyes; white felt pads; limited edition of 100; 1993.
Marks: Tag on foot; tag in back seam
Price: Current sales price

Steiff
English Club Bear
10 inches

Pale blue *Teddy Baby*; for the English Steiff Club only; mint-in-box; 1992 edition.
Marks: Brass button; white ear tag; porcelain Steiff Club chest ornament on collar
Price: $400 up

Steiff DisneyWorld Bears • 12 inches

Black bears with Mickey and Minnie Mouse masks; limited edition of 1,500 each; Mickey 1991; Minnie 1992.

Price: $450 up each

Lorraine Oakley Collection

Steiff Club Bear Sam • 11 inches

Premiere American edition; gold mohair; wears red, white and blue ribbon with a porcelain medallion; may be purchased by club members only; 1993/1994.

Price: $195 at issue

Steiff Club Bear Teddy Clown • 11 inches

Replica of 1928 bear; tipped mohair; ruff and hat; porcelain chest medallion; may be purchased by club members only; 1993 edition.

Price: $225 at issue

Disneyland Teddy Bears
24 and 12 inches

Large bear made in a limited edition of only 20; features two music boxes;
smaller bear in a quantity of 3,500 and has a single music box; each comes with
an enamel and painted metal souvenir pin; 1993 convention.
Marks: Button and tag in ears; printed commemorative ribbons
Price: $2,500 up (24 inches) $325 (12 inches)

The teddy bears that fall into this category present a wide and varied selection. They run the gamut in aesthetics and price, as well. A perfectly executed Schuco compact bear with its ingenious engineering or a muff with an attached head and legs can surely be considered innovative. There are also teddies that can be purchased for about $20 that present a holiday theme; these, too, can be considered novelties. The choices can be awe-inspiring or just plain fun.

Smokey
12 inches

Brown plush; nonremovable jeans and belt; velour hat; made by Three Bears, Inc.; 1985.

Marks: Label in seam; paper hang tag

Price: $45-$50

Barbara Yusa Collection

American Teddy Bear Muff
14 inches

White mohair; glass eyes; fabric nose; felt hands and pads; excelsior stuffed head, hands and feet; cotton lined; cotton cord to hang around neck; circa 1910; mint.
Marks: Sewn inside label: "Ideal Baby Mine"
Price: $1200-$1300

Fabric Teddy Bear • 23 by 36 inches
"Big Teddy Bear Cut Out"; © 1913 by Saalfield Publishing Co., Akron, Ohio; with printed instructions and two 5-inch baby bears.
Marks: As stated

Finished Hand-Sewn Teddy Bear
19 inches
Bear made from the same pattern.
Price: $475-$495 for both pieces

American Teddy/Doll
9½ inches

Brown coat wool body, limbs and hood; felt paws and feet; celluloid head; excelsior stuffed; all jointed; an attempt to create a combination doll and teddy bear; not popular when produced and, therefore, difficult to find today; very often heads (came in bisque as well) were imported from Europe; near mint; circa 1910.
Marks: None
Price: $500-$550

Bear Brand Hosiery Bear
9 inches

Oilcloth type fabric; advertising bear; a premium that was purchased as a rag sheet and cut and sewn by the homemaker; shown with Bear Brand Hosiery box; circa 1920.
Marks: Bear holds Bear Brand Hosiery box
Price: $165-$175

Schuco Perfume Bottle Teddy Bear • 5 inches

Pale gold mohair; metal armature; metal bead eyes; jointed limbs; head lifts off to reveal glass perfume bottle; circa 1925.

Marks: None

Price: $450 up

Schuco Yes/No Teddy Bear • 5 inches

Gold mohair; metal armature; inoperable because tail missing; circa 1925.

Marks: None

Price: $150-$200

Barbara Yusa Collection

Novelty Teddy Bear 3½ inches

Gold mohair; bead eyes; pin-jointed; attached is a small bottle of Canadian Rye; souvenir of Calgary, Canada; probably of German origin; circa 1940.

Marks: As stated

Price: $100-$125

Trudi Topsy Turvy Bear/Rabbit • 10 inches

Teddy bear with mohair head and paws; glass eyes; excelsior stuffed; dressed in blue and white gingham; turn over for rabbit with plush head and paws; dressed in red and white gingham; mint; circa 1960.

Marks: "Trudi" hang tag on rabbit

Price: $325

The Three Bears • 12, 10 and 8 inches

Cotton, felt and embroidered features; cotton filling; appear to be homemade, possibly from a commercial pattern; circa 1935.

Marks: None

Price: $35-$45 set

Steiff Zotty Pajama Bag • 16 inches

Brown tipped plush; inset mohair muzzle; glass eyes; head firmly stuffed; opens at bottom to hold night wear; Velcro closing; mint; 1970s.
Marks: Incised button; split chest tag
Price: $95

English Teddy Pajama Bag
15 inches

Gold mohair; glass eyes; rexine pads; swivel head; zippered back with quilted lining to hold night wear; excellent condition; made by Alpha Farnell; circa 1955.
Marks: Sewn-in label on leg
Price: $350-$375

Dudley Furskin
22 inches

Plush; unjointed; child-size clothes and shoes; comes with story book; Xavier Roberts Original; 1980s.
Marks: Label on overalls; hang tag booklet
Price: $65-$70
Lorraine Oakley Collection

Nisbet Zodiac Bears • 13 inches

Plush; plastic eyes; velvet pads; soft stuffed; all jointed; three of a series of 12; *Scorpio, Aquarius* and *Leo* shown; each dressed and accessorized nicely; taken from the book by Peter Bull and Pauline McMillan; limited edition of 1,000 each; House of Nisbet Ltd., England; 1985.
Marks: Satin label on foot; label with edition number in side seam; hang tag

Price: $250 up each

Barbara Yusa Collection

Hallmark Winter Snowbeary 17 inches

White plush; unjointed; soft stuffed; wears mittens and scarf; © Hallmark; made in China; 1980s.
Marks: Label in seam; hang tag attached to shoulder
Price: $45-$50

Hallmark Valentine Bear 8 inches

White plush; unjointed; soft stuffed; red ribbon; carries cardboard Valentine box; © 1989 Graphics International.
Marks: Two labels in leg seam
Price: $30-$35   *Barbara Yusa Collection*

Teddy Head Coat Hanger
13 inches

Mohair teddy head on mohair covered hanger; plastic eyes; made by Felpa of Switzerland; 1980s.
Marks: Hang tag
Price: $95-$100
Barbara Yusa Collection

Snuggles Advertising Teddy Bear
10 inches

Familiar bear often seen on television advertising Snuggles® fabric softener; woolly plush; plastic eyes and nose; soft stuffed; nonjointed; made by Russ Berrie for Lever Brothers; © 1986.
Marks: Label in seam; paper hang tag
Price: $10-$15
Barbara Yusa Collection

Good Bears of the World
11 inches

Plush teddy bear available to members who present teddies to needy individuals; nonprofit organization; Dakin & Co.; 1980s to present.
Marks: Label sewn in seam
Price: $9-$10

Crayola Teddy Bear
7½ inches

Royal blue plush; nonjointed; wears sweater with Crayola® logo; made by Binney & Smith for Graphics International; 1985.
Marks: Label in seam; plastic hang tag
Price: $5-$10   *Barbara Yusa Collection*

UFDC Luncheon Teddy Bear Palmer
11 inches

Named after the Palmer Hotel, Chicago, where the 1986 United Federation of Doll Clubs Convention took place; made of 1950s mohair by Merrythought Ltd., Ironbridge, England; autographed on foot by Trayton Holmes (then Chairman of the Board). Bears are given as souvenirs and are included in luncheon ticket cost which varies yearly from $60 to $90.

Marks: Foot label; hang tag; label in side seam

Price: $100-$125

Donna Felger Collection

UFDC Luncheon Teddy Bear
8 inches

Woolly mohair made by The House of Nisbet Ltd., England, in a limited edition of 310 for the Anaheim, California, convention; wearing sweater and Peter Bull button; 1988.

Marks: Label on foot

Price: $90-$100

Donna Felger Collection

UFDC Luncheon Teddy Bear
8 inches

Mohair clown produced by Hermann in a limited edition of 250 for the Boston, Massachusetts, convention, 1987.

Marks: Three hang tags

Price: $90-$100

Donna Felger Collection

Teleflora
Novelty Bears
9 inches

Plush bears made for Teleflora Floral Company to incorporate in holiday season arrangements. Valentine bears have heart-shaped eyes; Christmas bear wears hat, scarf and toy sack on back. Circa 1990.
Marks: Sewn-on labels
Price: $18-$25
Barbara Yusa Collection

Advertising Premium
Teddy Bear
13 inches

Brown plush; plastic eyes; soft stuffed; made-on vinyl clothes; music box; 1980s or early 1990s.
Marks: Sewn-in label; "Dan Dee International"
Price: $35-$40

Annalee
Christmas Bears
10 inches

Eskimo bear wears felt clothes with synthetic trim; 1989. Nightshirt bear wears flannel shirt and cap and stands in felt slippers; 1988. Both have standards. Annalees are felt with wire armatures and painted features; highly collectible; investment potential.
Marks: Cloth tag sewn in clothes
Price: $75 up

A rotund little ursine sometimes referred to as "silly old bear" is surely the most famous and loved teddy in the world. The earliest versions by Merrythought, Addams, Woolnough and Agnes Brush are becoming increasingly more difficult to locate, but fortunately, contemporary products are offered and they are all quite wonderful. Many are issued in limited editions so expect to find price increases when they reach the secondary market.

The copyright has been held by Walt Disney since 1964 and several companies have produced under this label. The appearance of *Pooh* can vary also since the cartoon or the classic look so beautifully executed by R. John Wright are both available.

Steiff Winnie-the-Pooh 12 inches

Gold mohair; all jointed; wearing knit vest; made for 1994 DisneyWorld Convention; limited edition of 2,500; sold out before convention ended with many people disappointed in not securing one. Certainly considered one of the most sought-after products Steiff has made in recent years. © Walt Disney.

Marks: Brass button with stock tag lettered in red and the number of issue included. Came with Disney Convention enameled pin.

Price: $600 up

Christopher Robin II • 18 inches

Raincoat, hat, umbrella and boots; wears T-shirt, short trousers with suspenders under rain wear; mint-in-box; by R. John Wright; © Walt Disney; 1986-1987.
Marks: Label sewn on coat

Price: $1,900 up

Agnes Brush Seven-Piece Set

Owl, Pooh (with replaced top), *Rabbit, Kanga/Roo, Eeyore, Piglet* and *Tigger.*
The only missing character is *Heffalump;*
value increases with so complete a set; Circa 1955
Marks: None
Price: $2,000 up

Agnes Brush Piglet
11 inches

Cotton; glass faceted bead eyes; soft stuffed; made-
on suit is of a stripe rarely seen; circa 1955.
Marks: None
Price: $250

Winnie-the-Pooh
23 inches

Gold plush; plastic eyes; yarn
nose; felt mouth; soft stuffed;
unjointed; removable vest;
© Walt Disney; 1964.
Marks: Tagged
"Gund Mfg. Co."
Price: $75 up

Bean Bag Pooh
7 inches

Plush; unjointed; made by
Caltoy of California;
© Walt Disney; pre 1989.

English Pooh
8 inches

Plush; unjointed; red vest;
© Walt Disney; circa 1970.
Marks: Sewn-in label
Price: $55-$60

*Courtesy of
Cynthia's Country Store*

Bean Bag Pooh
9 inches

Plush; bean filled; made in Korea; ©
Walt Disney; 1980s.
Marks: Sewn-in tag
Price: $35-$40

Convention Pooh
15 inches

Made for the 1st Teddy Bear
Convention at DisneyWorld;
wears hat and scarf, conven-
tion logo and pin back button
commemorating the event;
© Walt Disney; 1988.
Marks: Label in seam
Price: $75-$85

*Courtesy of
Cynthia's Country Store*

Piglet • 13 inches

Velour; plastic safety eyes; felt inner ears and scarf; made-on suit; made for Sears, Roebuck and Co.; © Walt Disney; circa 1988.
Marks: Hang tag in ear
Price: $60-$70

Piglet • 10 inches

Plush; plastic bead eyes; made-on striped suit; shoes; excellent condition; © Stephen Slesinger; 1963.
Marks: Knickerbocker tag sewn in left side seam
Price: $75-$80

Pooh with Honey Pot 14 inches

Wears bib; has bee on ear; in presentation box with "hunny" pot; by R. John Wright; limited edition of 5,000; © Walt Disney; 1988-1989.
Marks: Sewn-in label; hang tag
Price: $395 up
Courtesy of Cynthia's Country Store

Eeyore • 9 and 12 inches

Larger size is a woolly fabric, smaller is velvet; both have button-on tails; made by Gabrielle Designs Ltd., England; © Walt Disney; 1993.

Marks: Hang tags; labels sewn in seams

Price: $80-$100 each

Gund Pooh
15 inches

Made by Gund for the 1991 DisneyWorld Convention; plush; unjointed; limited edition of 5,000; © Walt Disney.
Marks: Tag in ear
Price: $70-$75
Courtesy of Cynthia's Country Store

Pocket Winnie-the-Pooh and Piglet
5 and 2½ inches

A set by R. John Wright; made in limited edition of 250 for F A O Schwarz.
They are like the first series except they wear scarves and Piglet's made-on cos-
tume has sleeves. The presentation differs in that they are nestled in a box of
crinkled paper and a small booklet is included. They are named "Wintertime
Pooh and Piglet;" © Walt Disney; 1994.
Marks: Numbered tag attached to each animal
Price: $750
It is likely that by the time this book is published, the issue will be sold out and
the price will have increased substantially on the secondary market.

Walt Disney Pooh
8 inches

Plush; unjointed; removable velour shirt;
available at Disney Parks; © Walt Disney.
Marks: Hang tag in ear
Price: Current sales price
Courtesy of Cynthia's Country Store

Steiff Musical
Navy Goat
9 inches

Long and short mohair; glass googly eyes;
felt wired and padded horns; excelsior stuffed;
navy blue blanket with letter "N"; wind-up
music box plays "Anchors Aweigh"; made as mascot for the Naval Academy; circa 1955.
Marks: None
Price: $475-$495

Steiff Horses • 15, 12, 9, 6 and 5 inches

White and brown spotted mohair; glass eyes; three largest have open mouths;
two largest felt hooves; all with leather bridles; smallest has saddle; circa 1950.
Marks: Raised buttons
Price: $450, $300, $200, $150 and $95 up

Steiff Lamby 4 inches

Black woolly plush;
white top knot and tail;
green glass eyes; excel-
sior stuffed; original ribbon and bell; mint;
hard-to-find; circa 1958.
Marks: Raised button;
chest tag
Price: $280-$290

CHAPTER VI

Steiff Grissy Donkeys
15, 9 and 7 inches

Plush; open mouths; largest size has leather hooves and is hardest to find; 1960s until well into 1970s.

Marks: Raised and incised buttons; chest tags

Price: $99-$240 each

(depending on size)

German Donkey • 5 inches

Dappled mohair; felt ears; glass eyes; horse hair mane and tail; excelsior stuffed;
plastic bridle; possibly made by Hermann; circa 1965.

Marks: None

Price: $45-$50

Steiff Lamby
8 inches

White woolly plush; plastic eyes; excelsior
stuffed; original ribbon and bell; mint; circa
1957.
Marks: Raised button; chest tag
Price: $150-$160

Steiff Lamby
12 inches

Same description as smaller lamb;
circa 1965.
Marks: Incised button; chest tag;
F A O Schwarz tag
Price: $225-$245

Steiff Penguins
8½ and 5¾ inches

White and black mohair; glass eyes; felt beaks and feet; excelsior stuffed; earlier than common *Peggy*; somewhat hard-to-find; mint; circa 1945.
Marks: Raised buttons
**Price: $150
(8½ inches)
$130
(5¾ inches)**

Steiff
Tucky Turkey
6 inches

Brown tipped mohair; felt wings and tail; velvet head; metal feet; excelsior stuffed; of particular interest because of Paris store Label "Au Nain Bleu St. Honore Paris"; circa 1950.
Marks: Raised button; chest tag
Price: $275

Steiff
Chicken
4 inches

Tan shaded plush; plastic eyes, feet and beak; excelsior stuffed; mint; circa 1960.
Marks: Raised button; chest tag
Price: $65-$75

Steiff Birds
7 and 4 inches

Mohair colorfully airbrushed; felt wings and tails; metal feet; swivel heads; plastic eyes and beaks; mint; circa 1955.
Marks: Raised buttons; chest tags
Price: $275 (7 inches)
       $225 (4 inches)

Steiff
Lora Parrot
5 inches

Colorful mohair; glass eyes; felt feet;
vinyl beak; excelsior stuffed; mint;
circa 1960.
Marks: Raised button; chest tag
Price: $120-$125

Steiff
Cosy Charly Penguin
10 inches

Dralon; plastic eyes; swivel head; belt
beak; soft and hard stuffed; mint;
circa 1960.
Marks: Raised button; bear head
chest tag
Price: $115-$120

Schuco
Noah's Ark Owl
2½ inches

Plush; glass eyes; felt feet; mint-in-box;
circa 1960.
Marks: "Made in Western
Germany" tag
Price: $175

Steiff
Tulla Goose
5 inches

Gray and white mohair; black
plastic eyes; felt beak and
feet; excelsior stuffed; mint;
circa 1965.
Marks: Incised button; bear
head chest tag
Price: $145

Steiff
Duckling
5 inches

Yellow mohair; plastic eyes;
felt beak, tail and feet; excelsior stuffed; mint; circa 1965.
Marks: Incised button; bear head chest tag
Price: $125

Steiff Gull
Mobile
2-inch birds

White, gray and black
mohair; felt wings, tail and
beak; strung on plastic wire;
in tube; circa 1960.
Marks: Incised button
attached to tube; logo on tube
Price: $100

Steiff
Halloween Cats
9 and 3 inches

Largest is all mohair; smaller
is velvet with mohair tail; glass eyes;
excelsior stuffed; original ribbons;
mint; circa 1955.
Marks: Raised buttons
Price: $180 (9 inches)
$90 (3 inches)

Steiff Kitten • 8 inches

White striped mohair; glass eyes; excelsior stuffed; head moves by
levering the tail; fair condition; circa 1928. Marks: None
Price: $150-$200
Barbara Yusa Collection

Merrythought Marvelous Cat • 11 inches

Long white mohair; amber eyes set in head in such a manner that they follow
you; painted pink nose; swivel head; excelsior stuffed; a wonderful animal;
mint; circa 1938. Marks: None
Price: $300-$350

Steiff Siamy Siamese Kitten • 4 inches

Tan and brown mohair; vibrant blue glass eyes; felt ears; open mouth; excelsior
stuffed; original ribbon; tissue mint; rare; circa 1948.
Marks: Raised button; watermelon-mouthed bear head tag
with brown printing
Price: $450 up

Posy
Pet Cat
16 inches

One of a series of lanky-legged animals; gray plush; shoe-button eyes backed by flower petals; dressed in pantaloons, dress and pinafore; near mint; by Madame Alexander; circa 1945.
Marks: Dress tagged
Price: $230-$250

Steiff Lizzy Cats • 7 and 10 inches

White and gray striped mohair; glass eyes; upright tails; excelsior stuffed; ribbon trim; mint; circa 1965.
Marks: Incised buttons; bear head chest tags
Price: $145 and $185

Steiff Susi Cats • 4 and 5 inches

White and gray mohair; plastic eyes; excelsior stuffed; ribbon trim; mint; 1960 and 1970s.
Marks: Incised buttons; bear head and split chest tags

English Musical Siamese Cat 9 inches

Tan airbrushed plush; blue glass eyes; excelsior stuffed; key wind on bottom activates music box; excellent condition; circa 1955. Marks: Alpha/Farnell label
Price: $245

Steiff Floppy Kitty • 8 and 13 inches

Striped mohair; embroidered sleep eyes; wool and foam stuffed; red ribbons; mint; 1974.
Marks: Incised buttons; bear head chest tags
Price: $110 and $145

Steiff Siamese Cat • 9 inches

Cream and airbrushed mohair; intense blue glass eyes; dark brown mohair inset mask; brown mohair ears with felt inside; open pink velvet mouth; pink embroidered nose; three embroidered red claws; swivel head; excelsior stuffed; excellent condition; circa 1950.
Marks: Raised script button
Price: $600-$650

Steiff Fawn • 5 inches

Spotted airbrushed velveteen; black glass eyes; excelsior stuffed; desirable and somewhat hard-to-find; near mint; circa 1948. Marks: Raised button; U S Zone tag

Price: $95-$100

Alpha/Farnell Musical Fox
12 inches

Rust mohair; white mohair chin, chest and tail end; glass eyes backed with felt; swivel head; excelsior stuffed; music box activates from the bottom; mint; circa 1935.
Marks: Cloth label sewn on bottom "Farnell/Alpha Toys/Made in England"
Price: $495-$525

Steiff Squirrel
7 inches

Gray short and long mohair; glass eyes; excelsior stuffed; velvet nut; mint; circa 1955.
Marks: Chest tag
Price: $150-$155

Steiff Deer
12 inches

Fuzzy plush; glass eyes; excelsior stuffed; felt-covered wire antlers; near mint; circa 1948.
Marks: None
Price: $185-$195

Steiff Doe
12 inches

Golden tan mohair; glass eyes; excelsior stuffed; mint; circa 1955.
Marks: None
Price: $150-$175

Steiff Diggy Badger • 11 inches

Realistic airbrushed mohair; glass eyes; felt claws; excelsior stuffed; mint; badger on all four feet increasingly difficult to find; circa 1955.
Marks: Chest tag
Price: $295-$325

Steiff Fox • 20 inches

Orange and white mohair; black velvet ear backs; glass eyes; all jointed; excelsior stuffed; nose restitched in non-Steiff manner; otherwise mint; circa 1925.
Marks: None
Price: $850 up

Steiff Skunks
6½ inches in begging position

Black and white mohair; glass eyes; open felt mouth; airbrushed felt feet;
excelsior stuffed; rare; mint; circa 1950.
Marks: Chest tag
Price: $250

4 inches in begging position

Same description except paws are plain; harder to find than walking skunk;
mint; circa 1950.
Marks: Chest tag
Price: $200

6 inches walking

All mohair; glass eyes; mint; circa 1950.
Marks: None
Price: $175

4 inches walking

Mohair; glass eyes; mint; circa 1950.
Marks: Raised button; chest tag
Price: $150

2½ inches wool ball

Woolly plush; mohair tail; plastic eyes; jointed head; circa 1950.
Marks: Raised button
Price: $55

Courtesy of Debbie Anton

Steiff
Nelly Snail
6 inches

Brown spotted velvet; vinyl underside
and antennae; iridescent shell; glass eyes;
mint; circa 1955.
Marks: Raised button; chest tag
Price: $350-$360

Schuco
Yes/No Thumper
Rabbit
10 inches

Pale violet and tan mohair; plastic eyes
and nose; felt open mouth and teeth;
swivel head; excelsior stuffed; excellent
condition; hard-to-find; circa 1960.
Marks: Tricky tag
Price: $475

Steiff
Froggy Footstool
22 inches

Colorfully airbrushed mohair; realistic conformation; large glass eyes; excelsior
stuffed; metal armature for strength; mint; circa 1955.
Marks: None
Price: $595-$650

Steiff Froggy
4 inches

Airbrushed velvet; plastic eyes; soft
stuffed; mint; circa 1969.
Marks: Incised button; chest tag
Price: $100-$110

Steiff
Curled Fox
10 inches

Realistically shaded Dralon plush; plastic eyes; long fluffy tail; hard and soft stuffed; mint; circa 1970.
Marks: Incised button
Price: $125

Steiff Possy Squirrel • 3½ inches

White and gold airbrushed mohair; long mohair tail and ears; glass eyes; excelsior stuffed; mint; circa 1958.
Marks: Raised button; chest tag
Price: $95-$100

Steiff Perri Squirrel • 3½ inches

White and brown mohair; glass eyes backed by felt; double felt feet; excelsior stuffed; © Walt Disney; mint; circa 1958.
Marks: Raised button; chest tag
Price: $90-$95

Steiff
Maidy Poodle
9 inches

Black curly "astrakhan"
plush; glass humanized
eyes; excelsior stuffed;
red leather collar;
rare; circa 1959.
Marks: Bear head chest tag
Price: $495-$500

Steiff Dachshunds • 12 and 20 inches

Black and rusty tan coat wool; shoe-button eyes; swivel heads; excelsior stuffed; all jointed; small dog has original collar; circa 1910.

Marks: Printed FF button

Price: $550-$650 (12 inches) $850-$950 (20 inches)

Steiff Spitz 9 inches

Off-white mohair; shoe-button eyes; felt face, legs and ears; excelsior stuffed; shows some wear; circa 1910. Marks: None

Price: $350-$400 (in this condition)

Fox Terrier
12 inches

Off-white mohair; rust mohair ears; glass eyes; swivel head; shows some wear; possibly English; circa 1925.
Marks: None
Price: $75-$80
Doris Barrows Collection

Bing Trippel-Trappel Dog
approximately 8 inches

White and gray mohair; glass eyes; excelsior stuffed; jointed legs with wheels in feet; walks when pulled; original collar; leash and metal Bing Co. tag; near mint-in-box; circa 1915.
Marks: As stated
Price: $750-$775

Steiff Pip Dog
6 inches

Gold velvet (originally blue); tricolored googly eyes; felt tongue; horsehair ruff; excelsior stuffed; bell; rare; circa 1927.
Marks: Printed FF button; white metal ringed stock tag with "Pip/Steiff Original"
Price: $725-$750

Steiff Treff Dog
13 inches

Tan mohair; glass eyes; floss nose, mouth and claws; excelsior stuffed; mint; circa 1930.
Marks: None
Price: $550-$650

Steiff Bully Dog • 10 inches

White and orange mohair; velvet muzzle; large glass eyes; excelsior stuffed; swivel head; missing ruff or collar; circa 1930.
Marks: Printed FF button; trace of orange stock tag

Price: $800 up

Elaine Lehn Collection

Steiff
Dog Fellow
9 inches

Rayon plush; mohair face;
excelsior stuffed; excel-
lent condition; circa
1940.
Marks: Printed FF
button; square bear
head chest tag
with brown letter-
ing; tag on under-
side with "134"
hand numbered
Price: $295

Steiff
Sealyham
7 inches

Silk plush; glass eyes;
swivel head; excelsior
stuffed; collar; near mint;
circa 1940.
Marks: Blank button;
trace of white tag; water-
melon bear head
chest tag
Price: $575

Pajama Bag Dog • 20 inches

Black and white mohair dog in sleeping position; clear glass eyes; excelsior and kapok stuffed; zipper in bottom to hold night clothes; English; manufacturer unknown; circa 1930.

Marks: None

Price: $350-$400

Doris Barrows Collection

Steiff Molly Dog 6 inches

Long silky cream with brown shaded mohair; glass eyes; swivel head; excelsior stuffed; near mint; circa 1930. Marks: Printed FF button; trace of orange stock tag
Price: $225

Steiff Snobby Poodles in Wicker Basket
2-inch dogs

Gray mohair; glass eyes; all jointed; collars; flowers and ribbons; sewn to pillow in wicker basket; sold by F A O Schwarz and probably arranged by them; circa 1950. Marks: Bear head chest tags

Price: $400

Steiff Cocker Spaniel • 4 inches

Black and white mohair; plastic eyes; excelsior stuffed; jointed head; collar; chain and flowers on head; evidently decorated by F A O Schwarz also; mint; circa 1950. Marks: Bear head chest tag

Price: $100 up

Courtesy of Debbie Anton

Steiff Arco German Shepherd 9 inches

Shaded mohair; plastic eyes; open mouth with felt tongue; hard and soft stuffed; original collar; tissue mint; circa 1955. Marks: Incised button; chest tag

Price: $110

Steiff
Pulac Poodle
36 inches

Gray alpaca; glass eyes; excelsior stuffed; leather nose; long dangling legs in manner of *Lulac* (rabbit), *Sulac* (dog) and *Zolac* (bear), except this is larger; near mint; rare; circa 1950.
Marks: Raised button
Price: $950-$1,000

Steiff
Beppo
Dachshund
6 inches

Airbrushed mohair; glass eyes; open felt mouth and tongue; excelsior stuffed; all jointed; circa 1950.
Marks: Raised button
Price: $150-$175

Steiff
Waldi Dachshund
17 inches

Cinnamon long and short mohair; glass eyes; excelsior stuffed; original green collar; mint; circa 1950. Marks: Raised button; bear head chest tag
Price: $225-$245

Steiff Tessie Terrier • 5 inches

Beige mohair; plastic eyes; felt tongue; excelsior stuffed; original red collar;
mint; circa 1960. Marks: Raised button; chest tag
Price: $100-$110

Steiff Scotty Dog • 5 inches

Black mohair; tricolored humanized eyes; excelsior stuffed; red collar; mint;
circa 1955. Marks: Raised button; chest tag
Price: $215-$225

Steiff Hexie Dachshund • 12 inches

Tan mohair; glass eyes; swivel head; excelsior stuffed; original collar; circa 1958.
Marks: Bear head chest tag
Price: $180-$185

Schuco Lady Dog • 3 inches

Mohair over metal; glass eyes; all jointed; © Walt Disney;
from movie *Lady and the Tramp*; 1950s; mint.
Marks: None
Price: $125 up

Schuco Tramp
8½ inches

Beige and white mohair; rust velvet inner ears; black and white glass eyes; plastic nose; excelsior stuffed; ribbon not original; circa 1958.
Marks: None
Price: $155 up

Schuco Lady
8 inches

Tan, brown and white mohair; glass eyes; excelsior stuffed; embroidered nose; ribbon not original; circa 1958.
Marks: None
Price: $125 up

Both dogs: © Walt Disney's *Lady and the Tramp*

Steiff
Laika
7 inches

Russian space dog; white airbrushed mohair; excelsior stuffed; somewhat hard-to-find; circa 1965.
Marks: Raised button
Price: $325 up
(depending on condition)

Steiff Foxy Terrier • 12 inches

Airbrushed mohair; glass eyes; excelsior stuffed; squeaker; red vinyl collar; mint; circa 1965. Marks: Incised button; bear head chest tag
Price: $295-$350

Steiff Floppy Cockie • 8 inches

Mohair; embroidered sleep eyes on felt; cotton and foam stuffed; ribbon; mint; circa 1965. Marks: Incised button; bear head chest tag
Price: $95-$100

Steiff
Fire Brigade Teddy Bear
13 inches

Brown mohair; glass eyes; felt pads;
excelsior stuffed; hard rubber hat;
felt and leather belt; rope missing;
rubber metal tipped hose attached to
left paw; silver buttons on chest;
mint; rare; circa 1950.
Marks: Raised button; chest tag

Steiff
Fire Brigade Doll
17 inches

Rubber head; glass eyes; felt
body and clothes; leather boots
and belt; plastic hat; rope and
axe attached to belt back;
mint; rare; circa 1950.
Marks: Raised button; hand-
written ear stock tag; card in
jacket reads "Gruss Gott/ich
Komn Von/Albert
Ziegler/Schlauchund/Feuer
loschgerate fabric/Giengen
Brenz/Gegr. 189-
Fernruf 103 u220"
Price: $3,000 up for pair
Private Collection

Steiff
Cocoli Monkey
10 inches

Felt with mohair head; excelsior stuffed; glass
eyes; bellhop clothes not removable; mint; circa
1948.
Marks: Raised button
Price: $525-$550

Steiff
Tyrolean Doll
13 inches

Felt; mohair wig; all jointed; cotton and
wool clothes; leather shoes; mint;
circa 1914.
Marks: Printed FF button
Price: $1,500-$1,800
Courtesy of Michelle Daunton

Steiff
Humpty Dumpty
4 inches

Felt with airbrushed features; shoe-button
eyes; jointed limbs attached to head; excel-
sior stuffed; very rare size; mint; circa 1909
Marks: Printed FF button; white stock tag
printed M B 12 Steiff original
Geschalt Germany
Price: $2,000
Courtesy Michelle Daunton

CHAPTER XI

Steiff Mickey Mouse • 9 inches

Velvet; felt ears; pie-shaped eyes; long whiskers; excelsior stuffed;
excellent condition; circa 1930.
Marks: Stamped on bottom of foot "Walt Disney's Mickey Mouse." Design
patent 82802. Margarete Steiff & Co. Inc. New York. Chest tag with
square-shaped bear and brown printing

Price: $1,600 up

Rabbit Wedding • 15 inches (plus ears)

Made of lambskins; glass eyes; kapok stuffed; jointed arms; meticulously dressed
in felt, silk and lace; cotton underclothes; bride and maid of honor
carry bouquets; groom has lorgnette; clergyman carries a prayer book;
made in England; circa 1935.

Marks: None

Price: $850-900 set

Steiff
Waldili Dachshund
9 inches

Rust mohair; glass eyes; nonremovable plaid
shirt; green felt suit and hat; wooden rifle;
mint; circa 1950.

Marks: Chest tag

Price: $325

Steiff Devil • 11 inches

Rubber face that shows typical deterioration; felt forms clothes;
jointed limbs; tail; letter and cloak probably replaced; mascot for
Duke University; extremely rare; circa 1950.
Marks: Raised button: U S Zone tag

Price: $500 up

(depending on condition)
Courtesy of Ken Yenke

Schuco
Yes/No Monkey
10 inches

Felt face, ears, hands and feet; mohair head; glass
eyes; excelsior stuffed; nonremovable clothes;
excellent condition; circa 1950.
Marks: None
Price: $450-$475

Steiff
Kiki Chicken &
Lixie Cat
4 inches

Yellow mohair; felt comb; plastic
beak; rubber boots; cotton clothes;
mint; mohair head; rubber hands
and boots; glass eyes; felt ears; cotton and felt clothes; boots slightly
melted; circa 1955.
Marks: Raised button;
chest tag
Price: $250-$275

Kersa
Rabbit
10 inches

Tan felt head and paws; black eyes; painted spots
by embroidered nose; felt and cotton clothes;
basket on back; tissue mint;
circa 1950.
Marks: Red tag in ear "Kersa U S Zone 203/35"
Price: $240
Private Collection

Kersa
Dwarf
16 inches

Felt molded face with painted features; white plush beard, eyebrows and hair; tan, brown and orange felt nonremovable clothes; excelsior stuffed; swivel head; mint; hard-to-find; circa 1950.
Marks: None (Prong marks on left sole where tag was originally placed.)
Price: $245

Steiff
Santa Claus
5 and 12 inches

Rubber faces (and hands on smallest) with minimal cracking; felt hands on larger; nonremovable felt clothes; excelsior stuffed; mohair wigs and beards; near mint; circa 1955.
Marks: None (5 inches);
Bear head chest tag (12 inches)
Price: $250 up (5 inches)
$550-$650 (12 inches)

Steiff
Gucki Dwarf
11 inches

One of three dwarves; rubber face; felt jointed body; cotton clothes; button and feather in felt hat; vinyl shoes; mint; circa 1958.
Marks: Plastic bracelet with raised button and stock tag; chest tag
Price: $135-$140

Steiff
Vincent Sheepherder
12 inches

Rubber face with mohair beard; felt body
and clothes; somewhat hard-to-find in
this size; shown with lambs described in
Chapter VI; mint; circa 1960.
Marks: Raised button; chest tag
Price: $250

Schuco
Mascott Minnie Mouse
4 inches

Vinyl and felt; bendable; © Walt Disney;
circa 1960.
Marks: Schuco logo on box
Price: $175-$195

Steiff
Max and Moritz
4 inches

Plastic figures from fiction along with
German edition book.
Marks: Raised buttons; chest tags
Price: $250 for dolls and book

Japanese Mechanical Bear in Bed
9 inches

Tin, plush, vinyl and composition; battery operated; off and on switch; when alarm clock rings, bear's eyes open and he sits up; mint; circa 1950.
Marks: Printed on bed "Mar Co. Inc. Japan"
Price: $350 up

Francoise Flint and Family Collection

Steiff Tumbling Bear • 12 inches

Tan mohair; shoe-button eyes; felt pads; excelsior stuffed; clockwork mechanism; wind right arm and he performs somersaults; shows mohair wear and operates sporadically; circa 1910.
Marks: Printed FF button
Price: $900-$1,000
(in this condition)

Mechanical Bear
11 inches

Rabbit fur over molded body; papier-mâché muzzle; wooden carved paws; glass eyes; open mouth; key wound; probably made by Roullet and DeCamp; circa 1910.
Marks: None
Price: $1,100 up
Francoise Flint and Family Collection

Schuco Tumbling Bear • 5 inches

Lavender mohair over metal; metal eyes; jointed limbs; felt pads; clockwork mechanism; wind arms and bear turns somersaults; rare color; mint; circa 1925.

Marks: None

Price: $850 up

Francoise Flint and Family Collection

Japanese Walking Bear 4 inches

Plush over metal; key wound walker; mint-in-box; circa 1950.
Marks: "Made in Occupied Japan"
Price: $55-$65

Bing Mechanical Duck
8 inches

Colorful mohair; shoe-button eyes; felt beak; metal feet; excelsior stuffed; key wound waddler; excellent condition; circa 1929.
Marks: None
Price: $225-$250

Schuco Dancing Drummer Pig
4 inches

Felt over metal; key wound; excellent condition; circa 1930.
Marks: "Schuco Pat'd" impressed on foot
Price: $350 up
Lorraine Oakley Collection

Japanese Mechanical Polar Bear
6 inches

White plush over metal; carries fish in his mouth and a seal in his paws; key wound walker; mint-in-box; circa 1950.
Marks: "T.T.T. Made in Japan"
Price: $75 up

Japanese Mechanical Drummer Bear
6 inches

White plush over metal; metal drum; when wound, bear plays drum; circa 1955.
Marks: None
Price: $55-$60
Dennis Yusa Collection

Steiff Mechanical Display
15 inches

The 1909 replica bear affixed to a plastic mechanized (electric) turntable; used for dealer display; mint; 1983.
Marks: Brass button; hang tags
Price: $525-$550

Russian Mechanical Bear
9 inches

Brown plush over metal; composition nose and mouth; key wound dancer; 1983.
Marks: None
Price: $40-$45
Doris Barrows Collection

Schuco Yes/No Orangutan 17½ inches

Rust curly mohair; felt face; prehensile hands and feet; glass eyes; excelsior stuffed; all jointed; circa 1950.
Marks: None
Price: $650- $700

Monkey
12 inches

Mohair simian with felt face,
glass eyes, and painted nose
and mouth; excelsior stuffed;
all jointed; circa 1960;
Japanese.
Marks: None
Price: $55-$65

Schuco
Yes/No
Bellhop Monkey
12 inches

Felt face; mohair head and paws;
rayon pawpads; glass eyes; cotton and
rayon clothes; all jointed; circa 1925.
Marks: None
Price: $250 up
(depending on condition)

Hermann Baboon • 4 inches

Tan mohair; felt ears, face and feet; glass eyes; excelsior stuffed; near mint; circa 1960.
Marks: None
Price: $35-$40

Steiff Monkeys
Gora 25 inches; Hango 11 inches;
Bamboo 12 inches; Bongo 18 inches

Softly stuffed and dangly plush simians; plastic eyes; 1980s.
Marks: Brass buttons; split chest tags
Price: $110-$285
(from smallest to largest size)

Steiff
Floppy Panda
12 inches

Black and white mohair; felt mouth; airbrushed felt feet;
embroidered sleep eyes; soft stuffed; near mint; circa 1960.
Marks: None
Price: $125-$135

Steiff
Panda Bear
10 inches

Black and white mohair;
glass eyes; felt mouth and
paws; excelsior stuffed; excellent condition; circa 1950.
Marks: None
Price: $850
Lorraine Oakley Collection

German Bear on Fours • 12 inches

White mohair tipped bright orange; brown glass eyes; felt pads; swivel head;
excelsior and cotton stuffed; worn condition; possibly made by Schuco;
circa 1925. Marks: None

Price: $65-$70

Ronnie Morrison Collection

Panda Bear
5 inches

Cloth body; celluloid head; excelsior
stuffed; pink ribbon; possibly Japanese;
circa 1945.
Marks: None
Price: $25-$30

English Panda Bear
21 inches

Black and white mohair; glass eyes; vinyl pads; excelsior and kapok stuffed; not jointed, but legs are stitched at body line making bear floppy and posable; red collar and chain leash; circa 1950.
Marks: Tagged "Dean's Rag Book, Made in England"
Price: $350-$375

Panda Bear
18 inches

Black and white mohair; glass eyes; open red mouth; excelsior stuffed; all jointed; appears to be German; mint; circa 1950.
Marks: None
Price: $395-$425
Courtesy of Dottie Ayers

Steiff Bear
9 inches

Brown mohair; tan inset muzzle; glass eyes; felt pads; excelsior stuffed; the head moves by levering the tail; one of a few animals made with this mechanism; mint; rare; circa 1930.
Marks: Printed FF button
Price: $2,500 up

German Bear on Fours
8 inches

Brown mohair; glass eyes; open felt mouth; excelsior stuffed; plastic collar; near mint; circa 1960.
Marks: None
Price: $95-$120
Barbara Yusa Collection

Steiff Panda Bear
20 inches

Black and white mohair; glass eyes; suedene pads; open felt mouth; excelsior stuffed; all jointed; near mint; circa 1955.
Marks: None
Price: $1,800 up

Schuco Yes/No Panda Bear
5 inches

Black and white mohair over metal; glass eyes; all jointed; levering tail produces yes/no action; near mint; circa 1955.
Marks: None
Price: $700-$750

Schuco Berlin Bear
3 inches

Brown mohair over metal; wears Berlin banner and metal crown; mint; circa 1955.
Marks: None
Price: $175-$200

Steiff
Polar Bear
8 inches

White mohair; blue glass eyes; felt soles on feet; excelsior stuffed; collar and bell; tissue mint; circa 1958.
Marks: Raised button; chest tag
Price: $350 up

Steiff
Panda Bear
3½ inches

Black and white mohair; plastic eyes; swivel head; bendable limbs; excelsior stuffed; hard-to-find; mint; circa 1960.
Marks: Incised button
Price: $195

Steiff
Panda Bear
on fours
7 inches

Black and white plush; plastic eyes; velour pads; soft stuffed; made to commemorate President Nixon's visit to China and China's gift of two pandas to the Washington, D.C. Zoo; 1972.
Marks: None
Price: $135

Steiff Panda Bears 15 and 10 inches

Black and white mohair; inset snouts; felt pads (bottom lined for standing); hard and soft stuffed; all jointed; reproduced from 1938 example; hard-to-find; tissue mint; 1984 only.
Marks: Brass buttons; chest tags
**Price: $350-$375
(15 inches)
$285-$295
(10 inches)**

Steiff Panda Bear 5½ inches

Black and white mohair; plastic eyes; soft stuffed; all jointed; ribbon; limited edition of 1,000 for Hobby Center Toys (now the Toy Store), Toledo, Ohio, to celebrate Festival of Steiff; 1980s.
Marks: Brass button; white stock tag; chest tag; hang tag
Price: $225-$235

Beaver Valley Panda Bear • 30 inches

Black and white plush; hinged jaw with molded teeth and tongue;
lockline movable limb construction; leather feet and claws; special order vest;
limited edition of 50; 1991.

Marks: Signed on foot

Price: $1,300

Lorraine Oakley Collection

Ivy and Brumas Polar Bears
18 and 19 inches

White mohair mother holding plush baby; glass eyes, firmly stuffed; to commemorate birth at the London Zoo; mint; made by Dean's in the 1950s. Marks: Tag on foot; paper hang tag
Price: $1,300-$1,400

Koala
2½ inches

Plush; plastic eyes, nose and feet; swivel head; made in Australia; circa 1992. Marks: None
Price: No price available

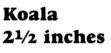

Italian Jockline Bears
9 inches

Brown and white walking bears; plastic eyes; molded noses; soft stuffed; 1980s. Marks: Label sewn in leg seam; hang tags
Price: $35-$40 each
Barbara Yusa Collection

Hermann Lion Puppet 9 inches

Mohair; plastic eyes; felt pads; mint; circa 1960. Marks: Hang tag on chest

Price: $55-$60

Vince Mirro Collection

American Bear Puppet
10 inches

Terra-cotta head; suedene paws; mended knitdress; collar with bow; possibly "Mama" of the Three Bears; maker unknown; circa 1935.
Marks: None
Price: $55-$60

Steiff Jocko Hand Puppet
9 inches

Brown mohair; white mohair beard; glass inset eyes; felt face, ears, paws. Note: *Jocko* in brown printing (first color used post WW II) and thick blue-lined bear head; common except with this ID and condition; tissue mint; circa 1948.
Marks: Raised button; chest tag
Price: $95

Kersa Uncle Sam Puppet
11 inches

Velour face; felt body and trim; mint; circa 1970.
Marks: Paper hang tag
Price: $75

Kersa Grumpy Man Puppet 13 inches

Felt with painted features; glass eyes; embroidered whiskers; wool scarf; mint; circa 1960.
Marks: Metal tag on body
Price: $60-$65

Kersa Pirate Puppet 12 inches

Felt with painted features; patch; brass earrings; mint; circa 1960.
Marks: Metal tag on body
Price: $60-$65

Kersa Mexican Puppet 12 inches

Felt face, hands, serape and hat; rayon body; glass eyes; embroidered features; mint; circa 1960.
Marks: Metal tag on body; paper hang tag
Price: $60-$65

Kersa Tyrolean Puppet 11 inches

Stockinette and felt; glass eyes; fur beard; mint; circa 1960.
Marks: Metal tag on body
Price: $60-$65
Vince Mirro Collection

Steiff Grandma Puppet • 10 inches

Vinyl face; felt body; cotton cap; plastic glasses; mint; 1980s.
Marks: Split chest tag   **Price: $95**

Steiff Chicken Puppet • 10 inches

Mohair; felt trim; mint; 1972.
Marks: Incised button; chest tag   **Price: $125**

Steiff Clownie Puppet • 11 inches

Vinyl face; felt body and hat; mint; circa 1972.
Marks: Incised button; split chest tag   **Price: $125**

Steiff Devil Puppet 10 inches

Vinyl face; felt body and hat; unusual; mint; 1970s.
Marks: Incised button; split chest tag
Price: $125

Steiff
Manni Rabbit
17 inches
(plus ears)

Airbrushed mohair; glass eyes; felt inner ears; swivel head and arms; excelsior stuffed; near mint; circa 1955.
Marks: None
Price: $750-$800

Steiff Rabbit
8 inches (plus ears)

Plush head, hands and feet; cotton body; glass eyes; swivel head; excelsior stuffed; cotton clothes; 1948.
Marks: Trace of U S Zone tag
Price: $375

Steiff Niki Rabbit
9 inches

Tan airbrushed mohair; glass eyes; open felt mouth; excelsior stuffed; all jointed; original ribbon; near mint; circa 1955.
Marks: Raised script button
Price: $240-$250

Steiff Rabbit
8 inches

Tan mohair; glass eyes; swivel head; excelsior stuffed; shows wear; circa 1930.
Marks: Printed FF button
Price: $450-$475

German Grisly Rabbit
15 inches

Gold mohair; glass eyes; clipped mohair pads; soft and hard stuffed; wire in ears; all jointed; mint; circa 1960.
Marks: Grisly metal button on chest; tag in arm seam
Price: $100-$120

Steiff Sonny Rabbits
3, 6 & 8 inches

Mohair; glass eyes; excelsior stuffed; swivel heads (except on smallest); circa 1965.
Marks: Incised buttons; bear head chest tags
Prices: $110 (3 inches)
$125 (6 inches)
$155 (8 inches)

Steiff Floppy Hansi Rabbit
9 inches

Tan shaded mohair; embroidered sleep eyes; soft stuffed; ribbon; tissue mint; circa 1960.
Marks: Raised button; chest tag
Price: $70

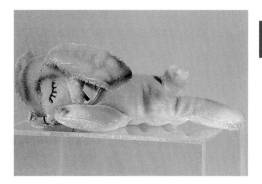

Steiff Floppy Hansi • 8 inches

Mohair; embroidered sleep eyes; wool and foam rubber stuffed; ribbon trim; mint; circa 1972.
Marks: Incised button; bear head chest tag
Price: $149

Steiff Lying Bunnies • 4, 6 and 8 inches

Mohair; black and white plastic eyes; velvet inner ears; excelsior stuffed; ribbon trim; mint; 1972.
Marks: Incised buttons; bear head chest tags
Prices: $139 (4 inches) $159 (6 inches) $185 (8 inches)

North American Hoppy Vanderhare 8 inches

Easter rabbit; one of North American's Vanderbear and Vanderhare Collection; 1990.
Marks: Label sewn to dress; hang tag
Price: $45-$55
Barbara Yusa Collection

Steiff
Nagy Beavers
10 and 4 inches

Tan short and prickly brown mohair; glass eyes; felt open mouth and teeth; smaller has felt paws and ears; excelsior stuffed; large size somewhat hard-to-find; mint; circa 1955.
Marks: Chest tags
Price: $180 (10 inches)
$75 (4 inches)

Steiff Dangling Frog • 13 inches

Yellow and green velvet body; large vinyl head with bulging eyes and open red painted mouth; soft stuffed; hard-to-find; mint; circa 1960.
Marks: Incised button; bear head chest tag
Price: $125

CHAPTER XVII

Steiff Flossy Fish • 11 inches

Gold and brown striped mohair; large glass eyes; open felt mouth;
excelsior stuffed; mint; circa 1955.
Marks: Raised script button; bear head chest tag
Price: $85-$95

Steiff Sea Horses • 11 and 8 inches

Colorfully airbrushed Dralon plush; glass eyes; soft and hard stuffed;
very hard-to-find; tissue mint; made only in 1959.
Marks: Raised buttons; chest tags
Price: $400-$500 each

Steiff Slo Turtle • 13 inches

Colorful mohair; plastic eyes; open felt mouth; felt claws; excelsior and soft stuffed; this largest size most desirable; mint; circa 1960.
Marks: Button; bear head chest tag
Price: $215-$225

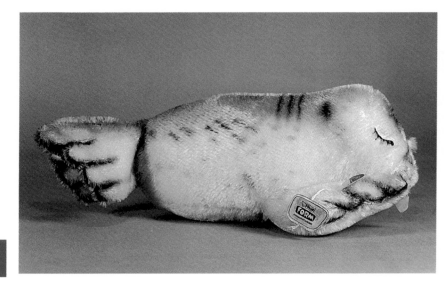

Steiff Floppy Robby Seal • 14 inches

Airbrushed mohair; embroidered sleep eyes; foam filled; mint; circa 1972.
Marks: Incised button; split chest tag; hang tag
Price: $135

Steiff Poodle 18½ inches

Black clipped and long curly mohair; glass eyes; open felt mouth with tongue; excelsior stuffed; circa 1912. Marks: Printed FF button
Price: $2,500-$2,600

Steiff Bear • 22 inches

Off-white mohair; shoe-button eyes; swivel head; excelsior stuffed; on cast wheels; note the head is more like a teddy bear's than the usual wheeled bruin; mint; circa 1908.

Marks: Blank button

Price: $2,500 up

Steiff St. Bernard 20 inches

White and orange mohair; glass eyes; excelsior stuffed; cast wheels painted bronze; circa 1910.

Marks: Printed FF button

Price: $1,500-$1,700

Steiff Elephant • 27 inches (plus trunk)

Gray felt; shoe-button eyes; airbrushed toes; felt tusks; open mouth; excelsior stuffed; bronze painted cast wheels; blanket and head ornament beautifully replaced; circa 1912.

Marks:
Printed button
Price: $1,800 up
Doris Barrows Collection

Steiff Bear 11 inches

Brown coat wool; shoe-button eyes; swivel head; floss mouth, nose and claws; excelsior stuffed; cast wheels; charming teddy bear-type face; near mint; circa 1910.
Marks: Printed FF button
Price: $750-$800

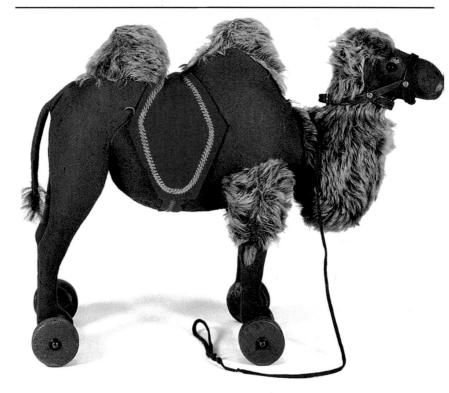

Steiff Camel • 13 inches

Brown felt with mohair accents; shoe-button eyes; excelsior stuffed; leather harness; felt blanket; wooden wheels; some mohair damage but overall excellent condition; hard-to-find; circa 1920.
Marks: Printed FF button; trace of white stock tag
Price: $795-$825

Steiff Duck 11 inches

Colorful felt; velvet head; shoe-button eyes; yarn pompon; excelsior stuffed; eccentric wheels; mint; circa 1914. Marks: "Steiff" imprinted on all four wheels
Price: $750-$850

German Bear
10 inches

White plush over papier-mâché; glass eyes; glued-on harness; tin wheels and harness trim; circa 1920.
Marks: "Germany" stamped on harness trim
Price: $400
Francoise Flint Collection

American Bear
22 inches

Cinnamon plush; replaced glass eyes; excelsior stuffed; on metal frame and wheels; rubber tires; collar and bells not original; repaired; unknown manufacturer; circa 1935.
Marks: None
Price: No price available
Doris Barrows Collection

Steiff Donkey
12 inches

Beige mohair; black mohair mane and tail tassel; black glass eyes; velvet saddle blanket; leather saddle and trappings; wooden wheels; near mint; circa 1928.
Marks: Printed button; trace of orange stock tag
Price: $850-$900

Steiff
Horse
5 inches

Tan spotted white mohair; glass eyes;
felt ears; excelsior stuffed; leather
saddle; plastic and yarn bridle and
reins; blue wooden eccentric wheels
that hop when pulled; hard-to-find;
near mint; circa 1950.
Marks: Raised button
Price: $195-$200

Steiff
Record Peter
10 inches

This is like *Jocko*; double felt ears;
hands clasp cart handle; when pulled,
cart moves up and down and bellows
under seat produce noise; mint;
circa 1948.
Marks: Raised button; U S Zone tag;
chest tag
Price: $395

Steiff
Duck
7 inches

Colorful mohair; glass eyes; felt beak
and feet; excelsior stuffed; eccentric
wheels; mint; circa 1950.
Marks: Raised button;
chest tag
Price: $125

Steiff Bengal Tiger • 24 inches

Realistic striped and colored mohair; green glass eyes; open felt mouth with four wooden teeth; excelsior stuffed; blue metal wheels with rubber rims; pull "voice" not operating; near mint Marks: Raised button

Price: $1,100-$1,200

Steiff Tabby Cat 8 inches

Off-white and gray striped mohair; green glass eyes; excelsior stuffed; eccentric wheels; original ribbon and bell; hard-to-find in this tissue mint condition; circa 1950.
Marks: Raised button; chest tag
Price: $350

Steiff Wooden Bear 8½ inches

Cutout silhouette; thick wood with brown wood-burned design; painted red wheels; pull string missing; circa 1970.
Marks: Brass Steiff logo affixed to side
Price: $100-$125

Steiff
Riding Ladybug
20 inches

Red, blue, black and white mohair; plastic eyes; soft stuffed; metal frame and wheels; rubber tires; mint; 1972.
Marks: Stock tag; split chest tag; hang tag

Price: $695-$750

Steiff
Riding Grissy
Donkey
21 inches

Gray airbrushed Dralon; glass eyes; felt open mouth; vinyl hooves; excelsior stuffed; vinyl and metal stirrups; metal rubber-tired wheels; pull cord never unwound; tissue mint; 1975.
Marks: Incised button; split chest tag; hang tag

Price: $650-$700

Steiff
Zotty Rock and
Roll Bear
24 inches

Plush; lying on back; metal rocker that also has wheels that can be let down; 1985.
Marks: Brass button
Price: $450

Steiff Elephant 12 inches

Gray napped wool; shoe-button eyes; felt tusks; embroidered toes; excelsior stuffed; all jointed; excellent condition; circa 1910.
Marks: None
Price: $750-$850
Dennis Yusa Collection

English
Jungle Toys Leopard
25 inches

Airbrushed alpaca; glass eyes;
swivel head; excelsior and
kapok stuffed; circa 1930.
Marks: Green paper chest
tag; sewn-on cloth label
Price: $325-$350
Fred Slayter Collection

Steiff
Llama
17 inches

Long curly mohair; glass eyes;
excelsior stuffed; largest size;
mint; hard-to-find;
circa 1950.
Marks: Raised button; bear
head chest tag
Price: $650-$700

Steiff
Elephant
3 inches

Gray mohair; glass eyes; felt
ears and pads; woven tail; plas-
tic tusks; wearing blanket with
Steiff logo; mint; circa 1950.
Marks: As stated
Price: $95-$100

Steiff
Lion Cub
9 inches

Spotted pale gold mohair; green glass eyes; excelsior stuffed; near mint; circa 1955.
Marks: Raised button
Price: $145-$155

Steiff Lion
Trophy Head
Plaque
10 inches

Wooden plaque with bronze plate; small lion head attached to top; probably devised by the Frigidaire Company for a unique presentation; 1954.
Marks On Lion: None
Price: $195

"TOP MANAGING DIRECTOR"
GROUP IV.
ROBERT B. GABLE
POMEROY'S INC.
ALLIED-FRIGIDAIRE
"BIG GAME HUNT"
MARCH, 1954

Steiff
Nosy Rhinoceros
11 inches

Gray mohair; glass googly eyes; felt horn and pads; excelsior stuffed; largest size of three; mint; circa 1955.
Marks: Bear head chest tag
Price: $200-$225

Steiff Bengal Tiger • 10 inches

Airbrushed mohair; black and green googly eyes; open felt mouth; four wooden teeth; excelsior stuffed; the model used as the *Princeton Tiger*: near mint; circa 1955.
Marks: Raised button
Price: $750 up

Steiff Bengal Tiger • 9 inches

Airbrushed mohair; green glass eyes; open felt mouth; vinyl teeth; excelsior stuffed; hard-to-find and desirable; near mint; circa 1955.
Marks: Raised button
Price: $375-$400

Steiff Leo Lion 25 inches

Tan mohair; long brown tipped mane; brown glass eyes; hard and soft stuffed; near mint; circa 1958.
Marks: Raised button; chest tag
Price: $595 up

Steiff Luxy Lynx • 11 inches

Gold mohair; bright orange eyes; black ear tufts; excelsior stuffed; mint; circa 1958.

Marks: Raised button; bear head chest tag

Price: $650 up

Steiff
Floppy Tiger
9 inches

Realistically striped mohair;
asleep eyes; hard and soft stuffed;
rare; tissue mint; circa 1959.
Marks: Raised button; chest tag
Price: $95

Steiff
Elephants
9, 7 and 3 inches

Mohair; largest has glass eyes and
replaced blanket; smaller two have
plastic eyes and trunks and original
blankets; felt tusks; excelsior stuffed;
mint; circa 1959.
Marks: Raised buttons; chest tags
Price: $175 (9 inches)
$145 (7 inches)
$95 (3 inches)

Steiff
Standing Leo Lions
11 and 4 inches

Gold mohair; long tipped mohair
manes; glass eyes; excelsior stuffed; large
lion has squeaker; small one has rope
tail; mint; 1950s and 1960s.
Marks: Bear head chest tags;
large has raised button; small has incised
button
Price: $225-$240 (11 inches)
$75-$85 (4 inches)

Steiff
Cosy Trampy
Elephant
7 inches

Gray plush; plastic eyes; velour pads;
hard and soft stuffed; plastic collar;
mint; circa 1965.
Marks: Incised button; chest tag
Price: $90

Steiff
Cosy Kamel
10 inches

Plush with airbrushed markings; plastic eyes;
excelsior and cotton stuffed; mint; circa
1972.
Marks: Incised button; split chest tag
Price: $145-$155

Steiff
Camel
6 inches

Wool plush and velvet; glass eyes; felt ears;
excelsior stuffed; mint; circa 1960.
Marks: Raised button; bear head chest tag
Price: $135-$145

Steiff Dangling
Panther
20 inches
(plus tail)

Black Dralon plush; plastic eyes;
soft stuffed; somewhat hard-to-find;
near mint; circa 1965.
Marks: Incised button
Price: $165

Steiff Molly Jungpanther
24 inches (plus tail)

Black plush with gray muzzle; plastic eyes; soft stuffed; mint; 1980s.
Marks: Brass button; split chest tag
Price: $275

Steiff Elephants
6 and 10 inches

Trevira velvet; plastic eyes; felt tusks; smallest has felt ears; soft stuffed; mint; circa 1970.
Marks: Incised button on large; split chest tags on both
Price: $115 (6 inches)
       $150 (10 inches)

Steiff Jungle Book, Series II
King Louie: 9 inches
Baloo: 12 inches
Bagheera: 13 inches

All made of cotton and acrylic; plastic eyes; soft stuffed; tissue mint; © Walt Disney: 1979-1982.
Marks: Brass buttons; split chest tags; booklets
Prices: King Louie $140-$145
        Baloo $350 up
        Bagheera $325-$350

Steiff
Studio Collie Dog
48 inches
(front feet to tail)

Magnificent example; long and short mohair; glass eyes; open felt mouth with tongue; excelsior stuffed; rare; mint; circa 1955.
Marks: Chest tag
Price: $2,800-$3,000

Steiff
Stamp
4 inches by 4 inches

One in a series of collectible stamps featuring Steiff toys; this one pictures a monkey, a doll and several sizes of gymnastic balls; stamp #8; circa 1920.
Marks: Printed Steiff information on face of stamp
Price: $155-$175

Steiff
Treff Dog
28 inches

Tan mohair; glass eyes set in head so as to form eyelids; excelsior stuffed; swivel head; mint; circa 1928.
Marks: Printed FF button; orange stock tag; bear head chest tag
Price: $2,000-$2,200
Courtesy of Michelle Daunton

Steiff
Studio Lion
30 inches

Gold mohair; long brown mohair mane and tail tassel; glass eyes; open felt mouth with four wooden teeth; excelsior stuffed; mint; circa 1950.
Marks: Raised button
Price: $2,200-$2,500

Steiff Tree House • 26 inches

Wooden cylindrical tree with simulated bark; three curtained windows; four perches; balcony; small door in front; opens in back to reveal three floors with fireman's pole to exit; sitting on 20-inch base; furniture missing; display piece; shown with various animals not original; near mint; hard-to-find; circa 1950.

Marks: None

Price: $950 up

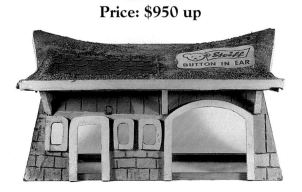

Steiff Display Farmhouse/Barn
27 inches

Wood with plaster and canvas overlay; used in shops to display farm animals; excellent condition; circa 1955. Marks: Paper label on roof

Price: $650-$750

Steiff Studio Badger • 28 inches

Shaded and frosted realistically colored mohair; glass eyes; felt claws; excelsior stuffed; rare; mint; circa 1960. Marks: Raised button

Price: $1,100 up

Steiff Mechanical House

Displayed at Festival of Steiff, The Toy Store, Toledo, Ohio, in 1991; molded houses duplicating an old world German village; electric; animals engage in a variety of activities; 1970s. Marks: Label on back

Price: $2,000 up

Schuco Postcards

Featuring teddy bears in outdoor settings; circa 1960.
Marks: "Schuco" on reverse
Price: $7 each

Steiff Hammer
11 inches

Colorful mohair: circa 1965.
Marks: Incised button; bear
head hang tag
Price: $90-$95

Steiff Kinderbuchs

Several Steiff animals were featured in books, two of which are shown here; animals with "Kinderbuch" on the chest tag refer to them being the subject in this book; books are illustrated, but photographs of the animals parade across top of cover; hard-to-find; 1960s.
Marks: Various authors and illustrators
Price: $25-$35

Steiff Shopping Bag

Steiff provides bags for their merchandise each year; this one appears to be from late 1950s or early 1960s; hard-to-find early bags.
Marks: "Steiff; Liebenswerte Spielfreunde"
Price: $30

Steiff Studio Hen 21 inches

Tan, medium and dark brown plush; plastic eyes; felt-covered wire feet; vinyl beak and mask; jointed legs; excelsior stuffed; circa 1972.
Marks: Raised button; split chest tag
Price: $495-$500

Steiff Anniversary Calendar

Calendar issued in 1980 to commemorate the company's 100th anniversary; in German, English and French languages; each month shows an early and a current animal; page shown on left is March with an old felt dachshund and a Waldi dachshund.
Marks: Steiff logos
Price: $55-$60

Bear Candy Mold
8¾ inches

Wonderful realistic bear wearing muzzle; probably European; circa 1910. Marks: Impressed "10779"
Price: $325-$345

Cotton Handkerchief
11 inches by 14½ inches

Red, black and white scene of performing bear with children;
probably German; circa 1880. Marks: None
Price: $125-$130

Victorian Greeting Card

Sensationally dressed white bears cavort across a folding card;
English; circa 1890.
Marks: None
Price: $65-$70

China
A B C Plate
7 inches

Brown and white alphabet around edge; center shows Mother bear and two cubs with "Wild Animals" at top corners and "Bear With Cubs" at bottom corners; English; circa 1880.

Marks: Triangular registry mark "IV/29/R/D/B P C; Made in England"

Price: $375-$400

Porcelain
Figurine
6 inches

Charming baby lying on a polar bear rug; German; circa 1900.

Marks: Impressed number

Price: $135-$140

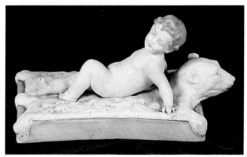

Child's
Tracing Board
9 inches by
11 inches

Lithographed children's faces decorate outside edge; frosted glass insert is removable so that subject matter can be changed; child places paper over the glass and is able to make a tracing; American; circa 1890.

Marks: None

Price: $90-$95

Polar Bear • 9½ inches

Lithographed paper; discs enable walking action; information about this bear
(Ursus Maritimus) is printed on back; patented in England, France, Germany
and America; Raphael Tuck & Sons Ltd., London;
circa 1900. Marks: As stated

Price: $150-$175

Three Bears Mug 3 inches

Charming scene of *Three Bears* out for a
stroll; *Baby Bear* pulls a bear on wheels;
English; circa 1900.
Marks: "The Foley China Co. England"
(later name changed
to Shelley)
Price: $150-$160

Bear Head Inkwell 4 inches

Colorfully painted cast metal; bear wears
a hat which lifts up to reveal glass
inkwell; American; circa 1900.
Marks: None
Price: $150-$175

Black Forest Bear Scale
6½ inches

Sitting carved bear in front of tree stump; brass gram scale; circa 1905.
Marks: None
Price: $175-$185

The Teddy Bears

By Clara Andrews Williams; wonderful illustrations by George Alfred Williams; Frederick A. Stokes Co., Publishers; 1907.
Price: $350-$450

Buttonhook
2 inches

Sterling silver; unusual small size; perhaps part of a chatelaine; England; circa 1907.
Marks: British hallmark
Price: $150-$175

Tin Litho Tea Set

Doll-sized pitcher (3½ inches), two saucers and one cup; charming scenes of children and teddy bear at the beach; German; circa 1908.

Marks: None

Price: $150-$175

Post Card Album
7½ inches

Bound in book fashion; each page holds one card; American; circa 1908.
Marks: None
Price: $45-$50

Print
15 inches by 20 inches

Colorful artist rendition of child and large teddy bear; entitled "Appeal for Teddy Bear;" American; circa 1910.
Marks: None
Price: $225-$245

Mechanical Clock
7 inches

Turn-of-the-century wooden clock; painted boy with teddy; when pendulum (not shown) swings, the eyes on child move back and forth.
Marks: "Made in Germany"
Price: $250-$275

Goofus
Glass Dish

Iridescent fluted edge; bear in center painted gold; American; circa 1910.
Marks: None
Price: $195-$200

Sporting
Bear Plate
6½ inches

Playing cricket; English; circa 1910.
Marks: "Tuscan China/England"
Price: $140-$145

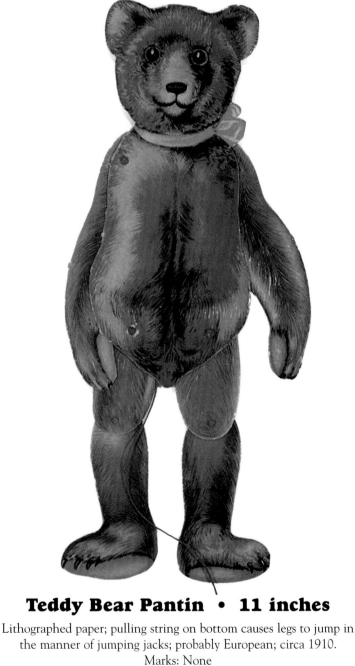

Teddy Bear Pantin • 11 inches

Lithographed paper; pulling string on bottom causes legs to jump in the manner of jumping jacks; probably European; circa 1910.
Marks: None
Price: $125-$150

Three Bear Puzzle
8³⁄₄ inches by 12¹⁄₂ inches

Cardboard 15-piece jigsaw puzzle; Father bear has caught a rabbit; Mother has picked flowers; Baby is in a tree surrounded by bees; probably American; circa 1910.
Marks: "4747 X 1" printed in lower left corner
Price: $45-$50

Happy New Year Postcard

Child kissing teddy bear; embossed with gold trim; 1913.
Marks: "Printed in Germany/series 767"
Price: $15-$20

Photograph on Fabric
8 inches

Sepia-toned photograph of a child holding an American flag with her teddy bear sitting beside her; cotton sateen fabric; rare; circa 1912.

Marks: None

Price: $250-$300